Ghosts of Lake Geneva

Rita Mae Moore
with R. Michael Huberty

AMERICAN GHOST BOOKS

CONTENTS

INTRODUCTION:
THE GHOSTS OF LAKE GENEVA

Often, one of the greatest questions that people find themselves wondering about, as far as the paranormal or supernatural is concerned, is how to determine if it's real.

How do we know that we are being haunted?

It's true that stories of paranormal encounters abound. While the grandiose tales of full body apparitions materializing before our eyes are compelling, the truth is that real experiences are often less…noticeable.

It's not the puff of smoke and brimstone, the thunderclap, or the shaking, bellowing screams that are the hallmarks of most hauntings. It is not dusty, tortured souls wandering along a hallway, shaking chains, conveying some urgent and powerful message. Instead…

Instead, most hauntings are subtle.

It's the chill up your spine. The cold rush of air that caresses your cheek when you're certain that there's no possible drafts. It's the quiet creak of a single footstep outside of your bedroom door when you know you're home alone. It's that inexplicable sense that you are being watched, with the urge to peek over your shoulder at every turn.

Real paranormal activity lives most often in that space of maybe. Maybe you left the window open, or maybe a ghost walked past you.

Maybe that doorknob rattled because a truck drove past, or maybe a disembodied entity is trying to make contact. Maybe that light flickered due to faulty wiring, or maybe it's the only thing a lost, tortured soul can do in an attempt to get your attention.

Maybe life goes on after we shed our mortal coil.

Maybe the other side is aching to make contact with us.

Maybe we are missing the clues, brushing them off as nothing, when in fact, it's so much more.

Maybe.

Lake Geneva, Wisconsin, sits just a few miles north of the Wisconsin and Illinois border, in the southeastern corner of the state. A small, beautiful town, Lake Geneva is well known as a premier tourism destination in the Midwest, earning it the title of "The Newport of the West"[1] in the 1900s. With its gorgeous lake, delightful assortment of shops and restaurants, and many activities, the city is a great stop for anyone to visit. In truth, since its inception, Lake Geneva has been a must see destination, ranking high on list after list of the best places to visit nationwide.

Like how Newport, Rhode Island served as the center of the wealthy New York City social scene during late Nineteenth Century summers (most famously portrayed in the Edith Wharton novel, *The Age of Innocence*), Lake Geneva served much the same purpose for the "new money" aristocracy of Chicago. One of the town's claims to fame is the fact that many wealthy families chose this site to build lavish mansions in the mid to late 1800s. Ringing the twenty-eight mile lakeshore, these stately manors provide breathtaking scenery

[1] *Lake Geneva: Newport of the West 1870-1920 Volume 1*, by Ann Wolfmeyer and Mary Burns Gage (1976)

for any visitors to the waters and the many of the families that built them are names that we still recognize today like Wrigley, Sears, Schwinn, and Maytag.

Modern Lake Geneva sees most of these mansions serving as summer homes but as the temperature drops, these homes stand essentially vacant, lending to an eerie atmosphere around the lake itself. One of the best ways to see these beautiful constructions in person is on the 28-mile footpath that circles the lake, created by the early settlers who believed that the first twenty feet of the lake's gorgeous shoreline should be public instead of private property. The trail was already partially in place, worn down over the decades thanks to the Potawatomi Indians who traded and lived around the lake. Shortly after the Civil War, the area quickly became known as a resort town with the influx of high society families driven by the need to live in their summer homes while Chicago was being rebuilt after the Great Fire of 1871. Once a railway line was constructed directly from the Second City to Lake Geneva, the small getaway destination became a premier stop in the Midwest and it has remained popular to this day.

The combination of creepy old mansions, wealthy and elite families, and the time period of the late Nineteenth Century cannot help but create a Gothic Victorian aura around the city. And no Gothic Victorian story is complete without a ghost. Lake Geneva has many ghosts, some perhaps merely legendary, but some very real to their witnesses and we'll be transcribing most of their tales here for the first time. From the haunted encounters of the Black Pointe Estate to the phantom red eyes of George Williams' camp, or multitudes of the rumors of strange occurrences at Otto Young's spectacular Stone Manor, the spirits that inhabit the stories of M.R. James or Charles Dickens seem to come alive in Lake Geneva as naturally as they did in London or on a manor estate in the English countryside.

However, it's not just the mansions that give the area around Geneva Lake such a spine-tingling history and stories of unexpected paranormal activity. The downtown area itself is home to many a sordid, spooky tale as well as the former locations of Lake Geneva's other claim to Nineteenth Century fame, their celebrated sanitariums, which were renowned nationwide at a time where Wisconsin was the mental health capital of America.

As tour guides with American Ghost Walks, we are ready to share these tales with you.

OAKWOOD SANITARIUM

LAKESIDE SANATARIUM

DR. WM. G. STEARNS, Supt.

CHICAGO OFFICE, 92 STATE ST.
Hours: 10 to 1. Tuesdays and Fridays

Oakwood • for • Mental • Diseases

Acute cases received for diagnosis and treatment. Convalescing cases re-educated. Rates as low as the most efficient treatment, and the best trained nursing will permit.

☆   60 ACRES OF OAK WOODS.   ☆

LAKESIDE

For General and Nervous Diseases.

NO MENTAL CASES TAKEN

Two Homes with complete sanitarium equipment.

Baths, Massage, Swedish Movements

Electrical and other treatments given to non-residents.

Training • School

For Nurses.   Two years' course

Special training in Massage and Hydrotheraphy.

2

While the history of Lake Geneva is often dominated by the stories of Chicago's wealthiest families and their fancy summer homes

---

[2] Sanitarium display at Geneva Lake Museum. Photo: Rita Mae Moore

even as early as 1912, whenever anyone wrote about the city, the next thing they would mention about this small town was the sanitariums. Idyllic Lake Geneva was not just a getaway for the jetsetter, but also known as a place for healing, where the ill could come to get better. These sanitariums specialized in "nervous or mental disorders" and their presence dotted the horizon and loomed in every skyline and view.

When you think about a sanitarium, you likely think about some kind of dingy, state-run facility, with tiny prison cell-like rooms. You picture hellholes where poor souls are left to rot by uncaring staff, abandoned by family to be forgotten. Many nineteenth century asylums were exactly that—dungeons where folks who were deemed "unfit" for society would be sent. It didn't matter if you were *actually* mentally unwell, you could be committed just on the word of a family member. Wives could be committed by their husbands for a variety of reasons from "suppressed menstruation" (lack of or uneven menstrual cycle)[3] to "hysteria." Doctors at the time thought there was a direct relationship between female reproductive anatomy and mental health. Hysteria and hysterectomy share the same Greek root, *hystéra* which means "womb." While women bore much of the brunt of "nervous disorders" of the Nineteenth Century, people born with disabilities or birth defects, as well as people with all manner of mental differences, would be sent away to asylums, where they would live a bleak and often tortured existence. The goal of these sites was not to heal, but to house, removing the "unwanted" souls from public view, to keep them "out of sight, out of mind." Often, what happened inside those sanitariums was anything but "healing."

---

[3] "Lunacy in the 19th Century: Women's Admission to Asylums in United States of America," Katherine Pouba and Ashley Tianen, co-authors (*Oshkosh Scholar*, 2006)

Lake Geneva sanitariums, however, were more like country clubs, and not at all associated with that dark and inhumane history. Instead of housing some nightmarish bedlam, the Lake Geneva sanitariums operated more like a rehab facility for modern celebrities, taking a month or two of rest from their ubiquitous "exhaustion." These facilities boasted scenic lake views, green sprawling grounds, activities such as horseback riding and theater, and cutting edge treatments. These were just as much of a high class hotel as they were a hospital.

Standing at the edge of what is currently downtown Lake Geneva, up the hill on Highway 50, a block away from where the Geneva Lake Museum now stands, was the Oakwood Springs Retreat and Sanitarium, one of the most famous of the Lake Geneva sanitariums. Opened in May of 1885, Oakwood was the dream of Oscar Augustus King, a groundbreaking physician who was a mixture of psychiatrist and neurologist. Originally from Indiana, King was an assistant physician at the Wisconsin Hospital for the Insane for four years and had attended lectures at the University of Vienna in Austria at the same time as the founder of psychoanalysis, Sigmund Freud.[4] He lobbied the Wisconsin legislature to pass the first bills regulating mental health treatment and it turned Wisconsin into the mental health capital of America. No other state had as many sanitariums in the late Nineteenth Century as the Badger State, and that is directly thanks to the efforts and vision of Dr. King. It also enabled him to open up his for-profit sanitarium in Lake Geneva.

This is why some sanitariums in southeastern Wisconsin weren't the inhumane oubliettes one might expect. However, since most of these places were state funded, there just wasn't enough funding in the budget to create a decent environment. Running his facilities for *profit* meant that King likely had a larger budget and thus, a greater ability to create the programs and treatments that were so very

---

[4] *The New York Times*, September 14, 1921

7

needed. However, only the wealthiest citizens could afford the help provided within. Those with lesser means were likely still relegated to the meager and miserable existences within less-desirable state-run asylums.

Dr. King's sanitariums showcased the most advanced psychological treatment in the world at the time. People paid up to $1500 a month to stay at the Oakwood Springs (that's nearly $50,000 in Twenty-First Century dollars), so they were getting the absolute best treatment possible. Although methods were becoming more humane than in the past, they still seem medieval by today's standards. In fact, one of the proudly advertised treatments was "hydrotherapy."[5]

Now, hydrotherapy doesn't sound that bad, in fact, it sounds like it might just involve hanging out in a hot tub, drinking wine until you feel better. Knowing that King, in part, chose Lake Geneva as the site for his facilities because of the beautiful lake, one also wonders if hydrotherapy there involved the lake waters. One proud advertisement for the sanitariums even beckoned potential clients to "come and take the waters." However, hydrotherapy wasn't quite as relaxing as it sounds.

Hydrotherapy did involve a bathtub, but that is where the relaxation ends. Patients would be wrapped up in linen towels like a mummy, and then soaked in ice-cold water. Others would be submerged for days in deep, narrow tubs full of ice water, only let out to use the bathroom. It was a cutting edge treatment for all manner of mental illness, and better than the lobotomies or electroshock therapy of the 1940s and 50s, but it still wasn't very much fun. The theory was that if a patient's core temperature could be abruptly and shockingly dropped, it would work to rebalance the "humors,"[6] which were, at

---

[5] https://lakegenevanews.net/where-troubled-folks-gathered/article_72536da2-3c07-5ece-bd34-f8fac4bcb9a5.html

[6] https://www.psychologytoday.com/us/blog/short-history-mental-health/201311/balancing-your-humors

the time, described as the ethereal vapors and influences that control the mind and body.

Of course, we know nowadays that that is simply not how it works. Dr. King ended up making his patients by and large cold, wet, and maybe even dead. However, he also treated some mental illnesses with marijuana, so it couldn't have been that bad, even with the ice baths. In fact, the *Lake Geneva Herald* in 1887 had a full article remarking on how nice it was:

"The cuisine of the institution includes in its season, the best of everything which our markets afford. Special attention is given to proper diet in each case. Out-door pastimes, excursions, walks, drives, boating, and fishing may be enjoyed by patients alone or accompanied by their attendants. Reading, music, dancing, games, and such other amusements are furnished in doors as are best enjoyed."

Indeed, Oakwood served up many ways of calming the mind and the nerves. Dr. King would marry an actress, Minerva Guernsey, and she often used her theatrical skills to encourage the patients to perform small plays. She would write, direct, and sometimes act alongside them. Patients were also welcome to go for walks, or even ride on horseback along the 63 acres that made up the Oakwood property. King himself was known to ride horses right along with his patients, encouraging them to enjoy the fresh air as much as possible.

Speaking of actresses and celebrities, it is a popular rumor that the famous actress Greta Garbo came all the way to Lake Geneva for treatment at the renowned sanitariums,[7] but that would have been impossible. King died in 1921, and while Garbo saw a psychoanalyst for treatment in the late 30s before her temporary

[7] "Mysteries of the Mind" by Lisa M. Schmelz, *At The Lake* magazine, June 2011

retirement in 1941 turned into a permanent one, she didn't even leave Sweden for Hollywood until 1924. Oakwood was on the way out by that point, eventually closing during the Great Depression.

As an abandoned building and grounds, Oakwood stood vacant for decades. The beautiful brick facade and ornate iron balcony loomed empty in the heart of downtown. By the 1950s, people were convinced that the site of Oakwood Springs was haunted. It became a place where local kids would sneak in, run around, and scare themselves. After all, it was literally an abandoned and creepy old *crazy house*. The most popular ghost lore tells of screaming coming from the building, even when there was no one in it. Passersby reported ethereal wails and cries for help echoing in the empty grounds, with no traceable source.

If you've ever played the game *Dungeons & Dragons*, you're familiar with the rich, lavish, and sometimes frightening worlds within the game. One of the creators, Gary Gygax, legendary Lake Geneva local, frequented the spooky Oakwood grounds as a boy. In fact, he credits the terrifying things he experienced within the halls of the abandoned asylum as the inspiration for the dungeon crawls of his famous game.[8] *D&D*, as it is called by fans, was born in Lake Geneva. Gygax's legacy evokes local pride. The Dungeon Hobby Shop Museum, opened in Lake Geneva in 2021, honors the game and Gary's influence on the entire genre of tabletop role playing games, and fantasy world building in general. Once the home of TSR (Tactical Studies Rules), the game publication company Gygax founded with Don Kaye, the building now houses vintage *D&D* memorabilia and hosts special game nights.

If tabletop role playing games aren't quite your cup of tea, perhaps current pop culture is. *Dungeons & Dragons* was the inspiration for the stories and monsters featured in Netflix's mega-hit show,

---

[8]https://www.gygaxmemorialfund.org/lgam-35

Stranger Things. Without Lake Geneva's fascinating history with sanitariums, perhaps we would have never experienced the compelling storylines in that show.

As far as the Oakwood was concerned, if it wasn't Gary roaming the halls and yelping with fear, it wasn't coming from any other traceable, human source. One hypothesis that might explain this phenomenon is the "Stone Tape Theory."

The Stone Tape Theory is the idea that events from the history of a place can, like audio or video tape recordings, somehow embed in the ground, bedrock, or even the walls of a building, especially in cases of extreme trauma or strong emotions. These bygone sights, sounds, feelings, and even smells and tastes then replay under certain conditions, becoming what we refer to as ghosts and hauntings. That's how old records work, you scrape a needle over a vinyl groove and you can hear the Beatles, for instance. Could the same thing be happening under natural circumstances, causing the wails witnesses hear? The Stone Tape Theory was named after a 1972 BBC television movie called *The Stone Tape* which was one of the first pieces of popular fiction to introduce this concept of a "residual haunting."[9]

The mentally ill are often under severe trauma, even if it's in their own heads. Certainly, physical trauma was experienced in those hydrotherapy ice baths. It doesn't mean the energy is dark or evil, and it doesn't mean that there's an intelligent, disembodied spirit wandering around, trying to make contact. The idea of a residual haunting is that this trauma becomes etched in time in the actual walls of the place. Much like magnetic tape, visual and auditory events become saved in their surroundings, replaying every so often when the conditions are just right (i.e., a dark and stormy night).

---

[9] *See You On The Other Side* podcast episode 107, "Stone Tape Theory: Timothy Yohe And The Paranormal Properties Of Limestone"

As much sense as this makes for the vast majority of hauntings, it probably doesn't apply at the Oakwood. After decades of standing vacant and multiple fires, the sanitarium was razed in 1959. Havenwood Apartments was eventually built over the property, which has only increased reports of weird sounds, footsteps, and screams coming from the property. Residents there, and even pedestrians passing by outside, often report hearing wails and cries for help. Even when law enforcement responds, there is no discernable source of the screams.

If these hauntings and ethereal sounds were borne from energetic grooves in the walls, the walls aren't there anymore. It stands to reason, then, that what we may be hearing at the site of the old sanitarium are actually the cries of the patients of Dr. King. Perhaps they never found peace in life because no one truly knew how to help them. Sadly their afterlives seem just as tortured.

MAXWELL MANSION

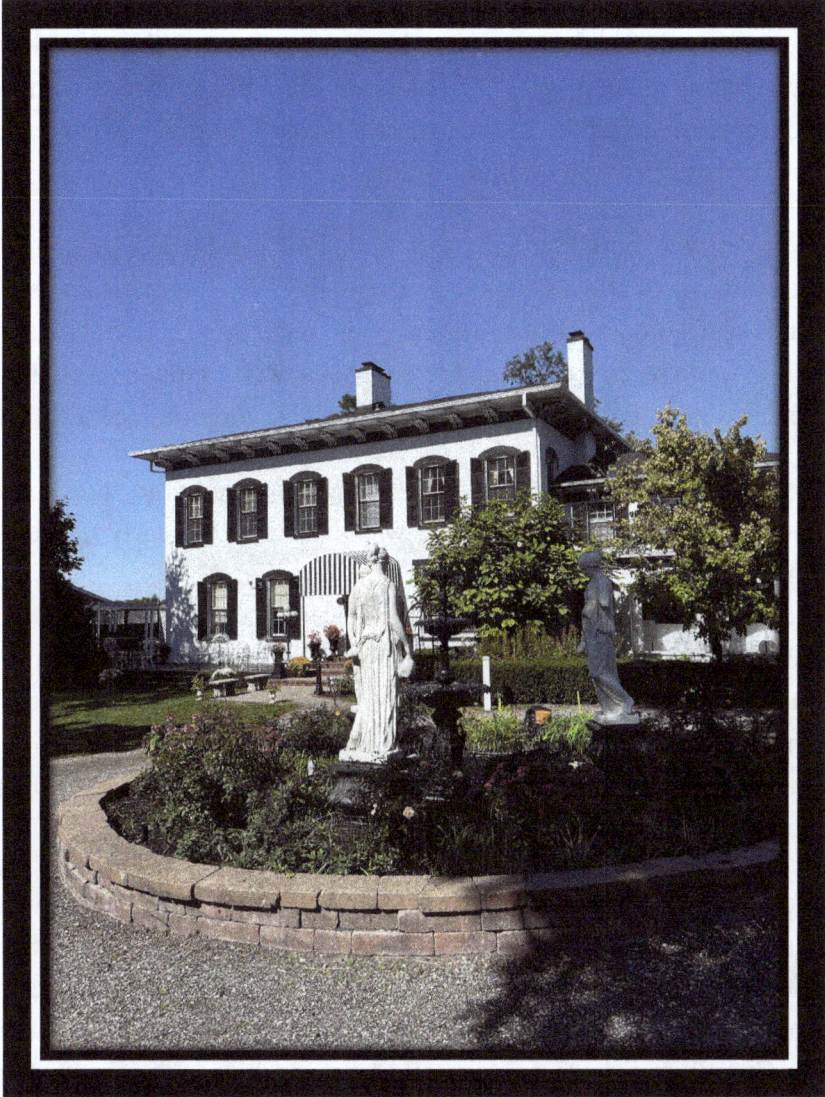

10

---
[10] Maxwell Mansion exterior. Photo: Rita Mae Moore

Maxwell Mansion stands just a few short blocks away from the lakeshore, and is a hidden gem in the city. Often, tour guests on our ghost tours with American Ghost Walks will audibly gasp in awe and appreciation as they round the corner, just past where the sidewalk ends, and step onto the front lawn of the mansion. Breathtaking indeed, with its beautiful fountain, striped awnings, and impressive facade, the mansion immediately gives off intense vibes of luxury, mystery, and intrigue.

The man who built the Maxwell Mansion was named Dr. Philip Maxwell. Maxwell was born in Vermont in 1799. The mansion itself stands as the oldest and the original grand manse in the Geneva Lake area. Prior to its construction, Lake Geneva was not much more than a small, sleepy fishing village, surrounded by gorgeous scenery.

Like many of Lake Geneva's summer residents in the mid-nineteenth Century, Dr. Maxwell was a pillar of the early Chicago community, but his notoriety began long before his life in the Midwest. As a young man, Maxwell served as a field surgeon in the United States Army, traveling across the country and treating injured soldiers. He had a knack for healing, and was well regarded in his station. Eventually, after his enlistment ended, Maxwell would settle in Chicago, marrying his wife, Jerusha, and opening a practice as a family doctor.

According to the *Chicago Daily Tribune* in 1854, Dr. Maxwell was considered to be a favorite to run for mayor of the city, and an 1872 edition even mentions that a sandstone bust was made of him in tribute on one of the buildings erected by the city rebuilding after The Great Fire.[11] In fact, Maxwell Street in Chicago is named after him—the street that birthed the famous market. When towns all over

---

[11] *Chicago Daily Tribune*, October 28, 1872, Page 3

Wisconsin and Illinois call their street markets "Maxwell Street Days," that's this Maxwell. He's known as the "Father of Lake Geneva" because he paid for the process of getting the city divided into lots and mapping it, so people could start purchasing land here and developing it. He was at the signing of the Treaty of Chicago in 1833, which established a truce between the United States government and the Potawatomi Indians, which was the beginning of Wisconsin and Illinois as part of the U.S.

Maxwell was a big deal, and not just in clout. He tipped the scales at 280 pounds and was known for just being a jolly fun guy. His reputation as a fun loving, hard partying, and hardworking man grew larger than even he was, and people spoke far and wide about his eccentricities. He's huge in the history of Lake Geneva as well as Chicago, and the tales that surround him are some of the most entertaining ones.

Maxwell started work on the mansion that now bears his name in 1855. He initially called it "The Oaks," in honor of the ancient, large oak trees that ring the property. Maxwell moved into this new home with his wife Jerusha permanently by 1856. Imagine the money and persuasion he would have had—it should have taken the better part of a decade to build a house as large and beautiful as this one during the 1800s, but after less than a year, it was finished. But alas, his time there wasn't long and he passed away in 1859, after nearly four years as a prominent resident. Maxwell died in the mansion itself, with his wife Jerusha passing away a number of years later, inside the home as well, after a battle with breast cancer. Both would be interred in Pioneer Cemetery, a few blocks away.

But, in the years before their deaths, the Maxwells would become well known for hosting some of the most lavish and entertaining parties. Maxwell knew well that money, in the Victorian era, was not made just at a job, behind a desk, or in trades work. He knew that the best way to grow and maintain wealth was in attending the fancy, high society soirees. True wealth was made in the handshakes and clinking of glasses at these events, in the deals that could be struck, lubricated with alcohol and entertainment. With that knowledge, Maxwell would host grand events regularly, inviting the upper crust of the Midwest to be entertained in his home.

Dr. Maxwell would also become infamous for his behavior at these events. He was well known to be the life of any party. At the end of the night, however, his personality really had a chance to shine. As the guests would begin to file out and head towards the stables, which stood on the back side of the mansion (and are now hotel rooms that you can stay in), Maxwell would follow, drink in hand. After bidding the final guest farewell, and when the final carriage door clicked shut, Maxwell would jump on the back of his favorite horse, drink still in hand, raised high to the sky, and he would ride, hell for leather, down the middle of the street, screeching in wild abandon.

It is rumored that during his life, Maxwell performed unauthorized surgeries in Lake Geneva in the basement of his mansion. Of course, being that the unofficial nature of these procedures meant that there would be no proper record, there is some uncertainty about the accuracy of this rumor. However, there's enough supporting evidence for us to safely say that Dr. Maxwell definitely *could* have been engaging in mysterious subterranean experiments.

Maxwell absolutely would know how to operate outside of a hospital. After Fort Dearborn in Chicago was abandoned in 1836, Dr. Maxwell proceeded to serve the army in Baton Rouge, Louisiana, and became the field surgeon for Zachary Taylor's military campaign against the Seminole Indians in Florida in the early 1840s. The good doctor most assuredly would have known how to provide healthcare in a makeshift physician's office beneath his mansion.

What kind of medicine might Dr. Maxwell be practicing? The discreet kind. Sexually transmitted diseases are a touchy subject in our modern sexually liberated times. In the mid-Nineteenth Century, syphilis was treated with the kind of fear and disgust that AIDS was in the 1980s.[12] It was a disease that wasn't fully understood outside of its spread through intimate contact and it carried the moral judgment that accompanies evidence of sexual promiscuity. The disease also could cause facial deformities, was often combined with open sores and pustules near the private parts, and was potentially fatal. This wasn't a toothache that you could just complain about to your neighbor or a malady like gout (a form of arthritis) that Benjamin Franklin could write a humorous ode to. And it's an oft-repeated rumor that the Founding Father himself had battled the social disease.[13]

So, the afflicted during the Victorian era would seek out an inconspicuous locale to be treated, and Maxwell Mansion would have provided the perfect setting. With a private, exterior entrance to the basement, no one would know who, or what, was happening below the surface. By the way, the reconstructive rhinoplasty used to disguise the deformations caused by syphilis was absolutely no fun.[14] Victorian medicine has historically been viewed as barbaric. With little understanding of contamination, surgeons often did not cleanse their tools between patients (after all, if you can see the results from the previous patient smeared across the tools and gowns, then you can confirm that the doctor is well versed in his trade.)[15] Without antiseptic or anesthetic, the patient would be

---

[12] Fisher, Linda A., "A Patient's Point of View Nineteenth-Century Syphilis Treatment" (2003). *Documentary Editing: Journal of the Association for Documentary Editing* (1979-2011). 351.

[13] "Ben Franklin," *The Office* (2007)

[14] https://www.empr.com/home/features/five-cures-from-the-past-that-are-more-misery-than-medicine/2/

[15] https://www.aamc.org/news/bloody-hands-dirty-knives-horrors-victorian-medicine

subject to a skin graft, with the forearm being stitched to the ruined tissues of the nose. After about six weeks, if the patient lived without infection or sepsis, the skin would be snipped, stitched, and formed to look like a rudimentary nose. With canvas or burlap up the nostrils to provide scaffolding support, the job was done, as gruesome as it was.

While we can't claim for certain that this happened in the basement, Dr. Maxwell definitely had the perfect location and skillset to offer these secret treatments. Rumors also persist that he treated a great many women that were "in a family way and did not wish to be." This rumor lives on by the persistent experience of women who enter the basement now. Known today as the Speakeasy Bar, the basement of the mansion serves up unique entertainment. As you head down the stairs towards the exterior entrance to the bar, you find yourself facing a large metal door with a small, eye level grate. You knock, hearing piano music wafting through the metal. The grate opens, and a pair of dark eyes stare out at you.

"Password?" a voice says, the piano music more audible through the open grate. You give the password, which changes weekly and is a loosely guarded secret in town, and the grate clicks shut, only for the door to swing open a moment later, permitting your entry.

Women who enter the bar often complain of intense nausea, dizziness, and discomfort. The feelings can be quite oppressive, and the women afflicted only find relief when they exit the bar and come up to ground level for fresh air. The general explanation is that these women are sensitive to the horrors that occurred a century prior within those cold, stone walls.

Now the idea that Philip Maxwell might have been some kind of mad doctor performing operations does add to the mystique of the Maxwell Mansion. In truth, though, a building that's over 160 years old, has had several different owners, and has had thousands of people sleep in its rooms, including historic figures in their own right like Nancy Davis before she became Nancy Reagan, and General and President Ulysses S. Grant, doesn't even need rumors to contribute to the haunted energy of the place. One step on the property is all that anyone needs to feel that strange energy.

It's also true that Maxwell developed quite a large reputation for being eccentric, which only served to further the rumor mongers who whispered about the strange happenings within his home. With every fancy party, even as the guest lists continued to stand as the most coveted to be upon, rumors about the strange doctor would swirl and spread. Even as Maxwell contributed great things to the Midwest, as both Chicago and Lake Geneva grew along with his influence, strangeness still was spoken about.

Upon both the death of Dr. Maxwell and the later passing of Jerusha, however, it becomes apparent just how important this small family was to the community. Their wakes filled the mansion with people, with some reports describing the crowd as so large that it spilled out onto the lawn and down the street. Both Dr. and Mrs. Maxwell would be buried in Pioneer Cemetery, just North of the downtown blocks of Lake Geneva. Their legacies as keystones in town linger on, as well as a great many strange tales about their lives, and their home.

In an interview with the former head butler, Jonathan Mindham, many unusual stories came to light. The new-at-the-time owners took over the property in the early 2000s, and began a process of renovation to bring it up to date as a bed and breakfast and event space. The butler was staying over alone at the property as part of his work duties, in what's currently an office, but at the time was a little apartment above the kitchen. His job was to be a caretaker, staying in the empty property to make sure everything was secure during the construction. As it grew darker and darker and night finally fell, he finished tidying up and checking things. He reclined into his bed and started watching TV. There is a tiny gap under the door out into the hallway, and he described in detail how the hallway light was on, but his room was dark except for the television. He then heard footsteps—heavy, slow footsteps, coming closer and closer to his room. These slow, deliberate footsteps echoed down the hall. He sat up with alarm and looked at his door. Backlit by the hallway light, he was shocked to see the shadowy outline of two feet step up to his door, just visible through the gap. He walked over to the door, said "Hello?" and opened it up, only to find himself confronting an empty hallway.

But as soon as he sat down, he heard the heavy footsteps again and saw the outline of the shadowy feet deliberately step up and pause on the other side of his door. He jumped up and threw open the door, and again, he found himself facing a completely empty hallway. The butler, frightened, called his friend on a cellphone to come over and help him check the property, and to distract him from what he felt was a case of anxiety and overactive imagination. He decided he didn't want to wait inside his bedroom any longer, with the energy around him feeling more and more alive and electric. He went down the main stairs, and was walking through the kitchen when he saw something in the main room. It was at the end of the hallway in the room leading to the main staircase where he saw what he describes as a shadow person standing there, a full-body apparition that was completely black.

He didn't wait around to see what the shadow was doing.

He ran out of the house, out across the lawn, and to the alley across the street, where he waited for his friend to arrive. Eventually she did, and they walked the grounds together, but nothing tried to make further contact with them. He stated that the energy and uncomfortable feeling had dissipated upon her arrival. She decided to stay over at the mansion, perhaps at his panicked urging, and noted that absolutely nothing strange happened as they prepared to sleep.

In the middle of the night, she woke the butler up, telling him that she did think that there was someone in the house. Panicked, she said that she heard footsteps and movement throughout the place. Once again, they investigated and found no one. At least, no one visible.

The staff at Maxwell Mansion are not strangers to weird noises, and sometimes the guests have experiences as well. Guests who have stayed in the Louisa May Alcott Suite have left in the middle of the night because they've been too terrified, unable to even explain to staff what happened other than the fact that they want to leave immediately. Staff has heard furniture moving loudly in the Jane Austen Suite when there was no one else upstairs—the sound of chairs scraping and doors opening and closing. And it's in the Grant Suite, the largest of the bedrooms, named again because Ulysses S. Grant was a friend of Maxwell, where people have reported repeated tapping on their shoulder by unseen forces. One guest in the Grant Suite reported that their phone was aggressively knocked off the nightstand and their book moved to a completely different table.

While the Speakeasy Bar might be one of the most fun places at Maxwell Mansion, it's also down in that secret bar in the basement where some of the most weird paranormal events take place. The door that goes from the lounge to the bar is in the shape of a bookcase, designed like a secret door, to make it feel like you're at an illicit party during Prohibition. One afternoon, the innkeeper was giving a reporter and her friend a historical tour of the hotel. They came down to the Speakeasy and were discussing the history of the location. When they stepped through the secret door, emerging next to the bar, they all watched the door open and close on its own three times in a matter of a few seconds. But even though it's a fake door, it is a very real heavy bookcase, and a breeze wasn't going to make it move. And in the subterranean bar, where was that breeze going to be coming from anyway?

On a different afternoon, Mindham was getting the Speakeasy ready for a few guests, when he was in the same spot as the innkeeper was when she saw the door open and close on its own, just adjacent to the bar. A cabinet filled with glassware came crashing down on him suddenly when there was no reason it should have fallen. The legs were sturdy and solid, and it was not lightweight enough to fall on you as you walked by. The butler said it seemed like it was pushed. He also felt it was pushed by an unseen force that meant to harm him for some reason. Since that moment, he tries to spend as little time in the Maxwell Mansion proper as possible.

Dr. Phillip Maxwell's Mansion is full of surprises. There's the camera in the cognac room that is always distorting and full of static. There are shadowy, humanoid forms that people see around corners, but when they chase them there's no one there. It's a woman and her son that people sometimes see on the staircase, and it's their faces that are sometimes seen in the mirrors behind the Apothecary Bar on the first floor.

The little boy that is often seen is named either Danny or Eddie, depending on who you ask. He is a young child, and his face is often glimpsed around corners. This young spirit is the reason why staff at Maxwell places toys in the attic, and they swear that you can hear a ball roll across the attic floor when no one is up there. This spirit is also the reason why there are some local law enforcement officers that prefer not to respond to calls at Maxwell if it's not dangerously urgent—they say that they do not like when the little boy tugs on their pants as they walk up the stairs. More recently, female guests within the Apothecary Bar have reported feeling grabbed from behind, only to find no one nearby who could have reached out to touch them. They all reported the same thing—that it felt like a tug of a child's hand on the back of their pants.

When we interviewed Beverage Director Rene Ratchek she said that when it comes to Danny, he only wants to play and "it seems like if you don't acknowledge him or if you don't react to what he's doing he gets bored and goes away." But she did mention how he terrified one of their staff.

"He also went after our innkeeper at one point, and she was a runner and a screamer," she says with a smile, "and he went after her all the time. She went into the attic and put things away from a party one time and he blew a whistle at her. It was like an old-fashioned whistle that we didn't have in the home at all and she came barreling down the stairs screaming!"

While one of the other bartenders protested to us that he "doesn't really believe in that stuff," he did have an unusual story that started on an otherwise normal, quiet evening. He described how a commotion began upstairs, in one of the guest suites. Staff assumed that it was a guest, intoxicated, causing damage to the room, but a quick check of the logs showed that the room was not booked for that evening. A few employees, including the bartender in question, went up to the door to knock. When they arrived, they were shocked to hear a series of loud crashes and bangs. He described it as sounding as though someone was tearing the room apart. When another staff member brought a key to gain entry to the room, they were all horrified to watch as the key sheared off inside the lock, broken clean off as though it had been melted. Eventually, they were able to pry the jammed door open, and despite the cacophony inside a moment prior, the guest suite was silent and perfectly in order as they walked inside. It was as though nothing had happened whatsoever.

There's also a rumor that Maxwell himself hid treasure in the walls of the attic of his mansion, but nothing has been found yet. There's still plenty of weirdness that goes on in this building, being that it is one of the oldest in the city, built before all the other great cottages and summer palaces. When it comes to haunted Victorian mansions of the Chicago elite in Lake Geneva, the Maxwell Mansion is the original.

BAKER HOUSE

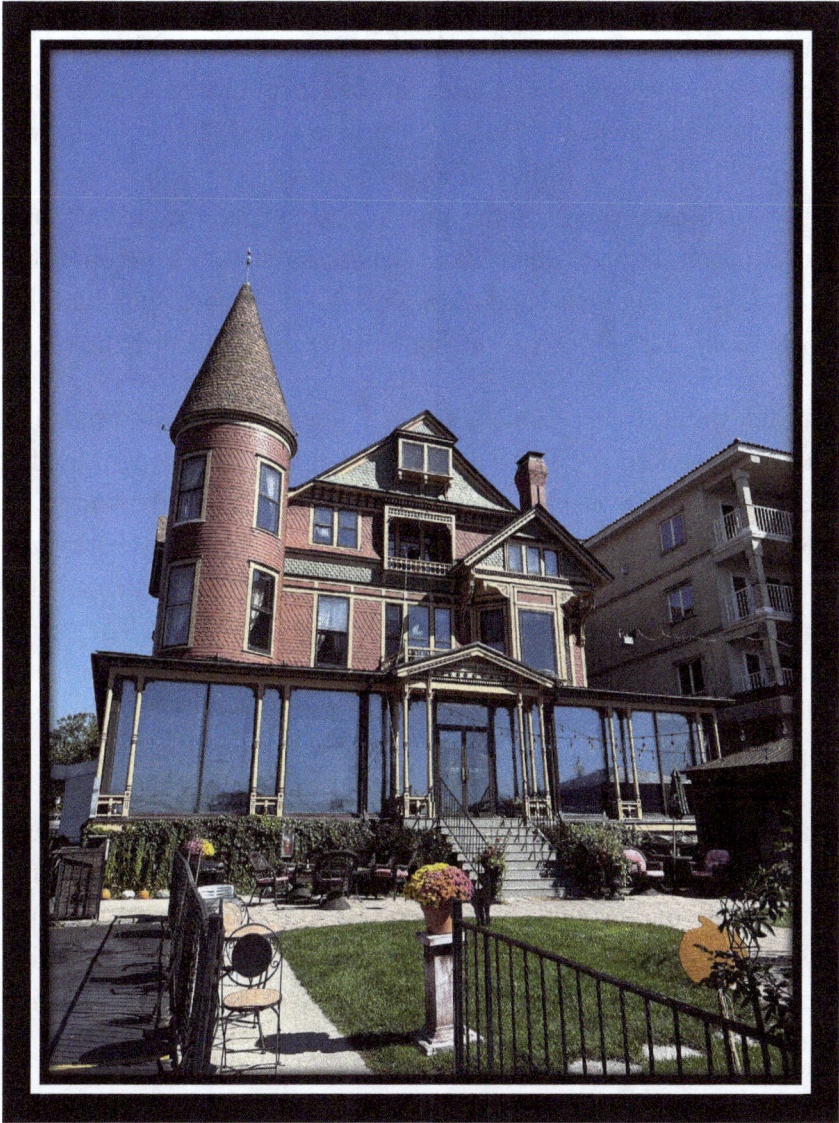

16

---
[16] Baker House exterior. Photo: Rita Mae Moore

The Baker House is a spectacular Victorian Mansion operating as a bed and breakfast right on the shores of Geneva Lake. It is high-end and comfortable and romantic and everything you would want in a weekend stay in a quaint little Wisconsin vacation town. Especially if you want something haunted.

The Champagne Suite is said to have the most activity. The suite, on the second story, is named after the beautiful champagne colored fabric hanging from the walls. As you lay in bed, the fabric will begin to billow and blow, although no breeze or wind occurs to cause such movement. Some guests have experienced the fabric indenting on its own, about hand height, as though some invisible entity is dragging their hand through it, lovingly caressing the folds of the cloth. Perhaps this is the hand of the spirit of Emily Baker.

The luxurious Baker House, as it's known today, was originally known as the Redwood Cottage, named after the trees who provided the wood for its construction. It was built for Emily, the widow of Robert Baker who was not only the former mayor of the nearby city of Racine, but a Wisconsin State Senator, and a man who made his fortune as an early partner in the J.I. Case Company. They even named the local high school after Case, a corporation that originally built tractors, and continues to this day as a global manufacturer of construction equipment.

The summer home was built for the whopping sum of fifteen-thousand dollars, and was completed in 1885. In modern terms, that sum equates to over half a million dollars. Unfortunately, Robert had passed away by that point and wasn't able to see the fruits of his labor, but his wife Emily proceeded to live there with their five adopted children.

Emily kept the house until her death in 1894. Over the subsequent years, the house changed hands numerous times, finding a bit of fame as a "paranormal tumbleweed," with no one person able to own it for very long. In turn, it served as a dorm for the nearby Lake Geneva Seminary for Young Ladies, which was located in what is now Seminary Park. The word seminary, in this case, refers to a finishing school for young women, and has no correlation to priests or religious studies.

After that, it was picked up as an extension of the also haunted Oakwood Sanitarium from our first chapter. Under Dr. King's tutelage, it served as the "Lakeside Cottage" where the building housed younger patients who had "lighter nervous disorders." King would also purchase the neighboring property, which was a white, three story, blocky building that he named the "Lakeside," using it as a sanitarium as well. The Lakeside would suffer a massive fire, and what stands on that site today is the Harbor Shores hotel. When King passed away, all of his cutting edge facilities closed down and were converted into homes and residences once more, Baker House being one of those properties.

After taking a turn as a sanitarium, it was a private home for a short time, owned by a supposedly mobbed up accountant who was rumored to have a speakeasy in the basement as well as a brothel. Eventually, the property settled into its niche as a hotel and it was known as the St. Moritz for decades.

The couple that purchased the Baker House in the mid 2000s also purchased Maxwell Mansion around the same time. These former owners, who have since moved on to other ventures in other towns, once lived on the top floor of the Baker House. And we were able to talk to them about their strange experiences as well as talking to their head butler, Jonathan Mindham, who split duties between Baker and the Maxwell Mansion. And it seems that the spirits in both of the houses loved to play tricks on him.

On his first day at work, Mindham had an experience that would serve to color his entire employment at the property. He came down to the basement where the staff changes their clothes into the period outfits that they use as part of the aesthetic of the bed and breakfast and after making sure that his costume was perfect, he glanced up and saw a man with a handlebar mustache, also in that same period clothing, through a window. The unknown man was walking across a room next to the changing area. He looked like a normal employee to Mindham, but didn't recognize him, and, being friendly, he decided to introduce himself. However, when he called out to say hello, the general manager abruptly walked out of the downstairs office and asked him who he was talking to.

"The guy with the handlebar mustache, I haven't met him yet," he explained, pointing just past where he had spotted the male figure. The manager, chuckling a bit, replied that that room was locked and there was absolutely no one in there, and furthermore, that they didn't have anyone on staff with a handlebar mustache. Mindham felt terrified and confused, unsure of how he could have seen someone that seemed so absolutely real, yet clearly there was no one there.

A short time after that, a housekeeper mentioned to Jonathan that she had a problem upstairs, saying, "that man is upstairs again". The butler was perplexed, unable to figure out who she was talking about. Checking the roster, he quickly determined that it wasn't a guest, and it wasn't an employee. Asking for clarification, the maid replied with a description that sent a chill down his spine.

"The man with the mustache," she said, and twirled her finger under her nose in the shape of a handlebar.

Three years later, "Handlebars" was seen again as Mindham was coming down a staircase carrying a tray of coffee and mugs. He was at the top of a short staircase where he saw the telltale handlebar mustache on a man standing at the bottom of the stairs. This time, it was different- the man was transparent, leaving no confusion over what he was. The butler, terrified, dropped the tray, broke the glasses on it, spilled the coffee mugs, and fell down the stairs. Quite a sight.

When Mindham got up, thankfully uninjured, "Handlebars" was gone. Feeling a little more brave, the butler ran after where he was sure the figure went, and toward where he thinks the ghost could have escaped to, but there was no one to be found. Jonathan proceeded to investigate the whole property and then asked the general manager to watch the security camera footage of the moment, because he's sure it would be caught on tape.

They watched the video and saw him look shocked, slip on the steps, and fall. They saw the cups break and the coffee hit the floor, and then they watched as the butler got up to run after... nothing. There was no one else visible on the security camera, despite the very real, traumatized reaction of the butler.

Who was this mustachioed spirit? Some wonder if it's not the ghost of Robert Baker himself, and others surmise that he's a long since departed butler or staff member that loved the property so much, he never left. We may never know for certain, even with strange experiences afoot.

That's not to say the security cameras don't ever capture anything weird. They are motion activated and will often turn on in the middle of the night, staying on for a long time, up to an hour, with nothing to show for it. Something moved that turned them on, but nothing appears on the image. Nothing, until a couple of years back when a translucent white feminine figure in a long gown faded into view on one of the cameras near the old servants' staircase. This beautiful specter proceeded to float across the room and disappear through the door.

Now, if your marriage is on the rocks, don't check into the Bordeaux Suite because it seems cursed to cause lovers' quarrels. Several couples have checked out early after staying in the suite because they started fighting too much. As they leave the property, most report that the anger they felt dissipated, with some couples returning, completely unsure as to what their original fight was even about.

Not bad at all for the "less haunted" of the properties that the owners purchased that year.

With so many different people in and out of the house over the years and so many kinds of people, from nuns to prostitutes, from the extremely nervous to mobsters like "Babyface" Nelson, who knows what kind of spirits are attached to this place. Or what kind of ghosts just had a good time and didn't want to leave?

One of our favorite personal ghost tales occurred at the Baker House in 2019. After a fully booked evening, one of the authors of this book and Lake Geneva ghost tour guide, Rita, had an oversold tour—that is, she took on extra guests and ended up with quite a large crowd weaving through the streets of Lake Geneva. Being the final tour of the night, they reached Baker House just shy of 11 pm, and the business was closed, with just a few staff members lingering inside to close up for the night.

She began her tale as usual, with her back to the building, facing the crowd. If you, dear reader, know anything about public speaking, you know what it looks like when an audience member is plainly not listening to you. Her entire crowd, almost immediately, was visibly not listening to a word she said. They were all staring at the mansion, not with an appreciative gaze for the beauty, but instead in shocked horror. She turned around to look at the house herself, wondering what she was missing, but everything looked completely normal to her. She shrugged it off and silently congratulated herself, because she *must* have been telling the scariest rendition of the tale she knew to cause an entire crowd to be visibly disturbed.

But no, after a few more moments, she saw that a couple of staff members, still dressed in their Victorian finery, were rushing out of the side door to the property and were running towards her and her group. She thought that was strange, as the tour has great relationships with the properties visited and spoken about, and all parties reciprocate the agreements of "let's not disturb each other." But, here they came.

"Hi Rita," the butler crowed. He was nearly running, with a very nervous look on his face. "We knew you were here!"

Being a bit of a sassy person, she smiled, gestured at the large crowd and then down at her portable speaker, and said, "Well, I wonder why!" He laughed nervously, as did the waiter that stood by him.

"No, actually, we knew you were coming before we saw you. We were upstairs, finishing up cleaning, when all of a sudden, every single door and window in the mansion opened at the exact same time. We immediately looked at each other and knew that you were coming, because the ghosts inside *really like when you talk about them*," he replied, completely serious. He explained that after the windows and doors opened, they looked outside and saw the crowd assembling as Rita was beginning to talk, her back to the house, completely oblivious. Many of the tour guests, however, saw the movements and were feeling perplexed…or downright scared.

"Well, good, I suppose," Rita laughed in reply. Better that the spirits enjoy her stories, than to have them upset!

Think about it. If you're a disembodied soul, if you're a ghost. What do you do all day? Sure, you get to spend your days haunting a beautiful old mansion and it probably starts out as a pretty good time. You get to fly around, walk through walls, and pop out from behind corners to try and make people wet their pants. How long can you entertain yourself causing the poor staff to drop trays, or to watch as someone senses you with a cold chill down their spine? Or you might like the sound of young people living their lives, after all it was a children's hospital for a bit and while that conjures a lot of tragic images in our heads, there might have been just as many cures and recoveries. There might have been a youthful positive energy for a long time.

Then, a century passes, and more. The people inside the building have no connection to you or your family. Fashions evolve. Cars show up. Planes fly overhead. The world changes. Strangers come into your home, oblivious to you. They do not know your name, or your favorite color, or the song that you sang to your children at night as you tucked them into bed. Even as they themselves lie in those same beds. You begin to wonder if you matter, or if anyone cares.

And then a girl in a corset brings crowds to stand outside your home, night after night, and you hear your name as she speaks. She tells your story. Memories. History. Acknowledging you and the people that came before. How you lived. How you died. What you loved, what you believed. Wouldn't you, once in a while, pop the doors and windows open to get a better listen? To remind yourself that you existed, that you mattered?

It's nice to think that may be exactly what is happening at the Baker House as our tour passes by.

FLATIRON PARK

Long before Lake Geneva was a tourist destination, it was home to American Indian tribes. The most famous of the indigenous peoples in the area were the Potawatomi, whose leader in the early 1800s was named Chief Big Foot. The state park that stands a few miles away from downtown was named in his honor. There are also high schools named after the chief, and Geneva Lake was called Big Foot Lake before it was ever called Geneva. The Indian population called it *Kishwauketoe* (Kish-Wau-Kee-Tow) which means "Clear Water." It wasn't called Geneva Lake until a surveyor named John Brink, a settler who made one of the first claims here, decided to name it after his hometown in New York State. Now that town was probably named after Geneva, Switzerland, a place both famous for its chocolate, and where the superpowers signed a treaty for the treatment of prisoners of war. A retreat on the shores of Geneva, Switzerland was the place where Mary Shelley dreamed up Frankenstein, so that lake has its own paranormal pedigree.

The Potawatomi settled here in the late Seventeenth Century after being driven from the East Coast by wars of the Iroquois Confederacy. After the Black Hawk War ended in the 1830s, even though they didn't participate, the Potawatomi population who had settled in Geneva were compelled to sell their land at the Treaty of Chicago in 1833, and were given three short years to vacate, eventually relocating once again to Kansas.

In the park adjacent to the lake, now known as Flat Iron Park, ancient effigy mounds of a panther and a lizard once stood. The mounds were twenty feet long, and about four feet tall. Unfortunately, as the new settlers built up the community, they chose to destroy the mounds in favor of quick growth and with a lack of respect for the previous occupants' sacred places.

Interestingly, the effigy mounds built on the lakeshore weren't made by the Potawatomi. The Mound Builders were an even older civilization that is still shrouded in a bit of mystery, thanks in part to the prolific destruction of many of the mounds all across southern Wisconsin as towns and villages were built up.

There are probably more mounds in Wisconsin than anywhere else in North America, and the builders of these effigy mounds were hotly debated by the early European settlers of the land. Newspaper reports from 1860 near La Crosse, Wisconsin describe the skeletons found in the mounds as a "race of giants," with thigh bones three feet long and two-inch long teeth. There were tales of a lost city an hour north in Madison, with estimates of as many as two hundred thousand people that once inhabited it. With a little bit of Nineteenth Century fascination with "savage" cultures, and the fact that these mounds were huge and all over the state, people let their imaginations run wild as to the ancient civilizations that might have created them. If it would sell, newspapers were more than happy to put those kinds of mysteries right next to more serious journalism. Picture if *Meet The Press* had a *TMZ* segment so that they could get the tabloid audience to watch as well. Writers and fabulists speculated it could be people who had escaped the destruction of Atlantis, or a European expedition lost to history.

Some even speculated it was the legendary "Ten Lost Tribes of Israel" who were cast out of Israel by the Assyrians in the Eighth Century B.C. This might sound silly today, but the "Jewish Indian theory" was taken seriously by famous Americans like William Penn, the founder of Pennsylvania. In the mid-Nineteenth Century, it was taken even more seriously by Joseph Smith, who used the idea of the Native American tribes being the lost Hebrews as one of the founding tenets of the Church of Jesus Christ and the Latter-Day Saints, otherwise known as Mormonism.

In 1894, archaeologist Thomas Cyrus put those theories mostly to rest with his impeccable research into the Mound Builders. To this day, mounds are still visible all over Southeastern Wisconsin (with one local mound being quite famously situated in the basement of nearby Lake Lawn Lodge in Delavan, with the hotel being built around it, but not destroying it). While there is still much to learn about the civilization that built them, one of the best guesses that archaeologists have is that the Lake Geneva's Mound Builders migrated north from Cahokia, a site near St. Louis that was a massive city a thousand years ago and the largest collection of mounds in the country. North of Lake Geneva, in Jefferson County, a site named Aztalan stands, with massive earthworks matching the Cahokia mounds. It is conjectured that perhaps the Cahokia tribes traveled north, stopping along the Wisconsin and Illinois border to build smaller earthworks, before continuing on to permanently settle at Aztalan.

While we don't know for sure how these great soil constructions came to be, we know that they have existed for thousands of years. We know that they still stood proud on the shores of Geneva Lake when Chief Big Foot and his people arrived, and we know that the Potawatomi integrated some of the mounds into their own folklore.

Now, the Water Panther, or *Mishipeshu*, was one of the most powerful beings in the Potawatomi folklore. It had the head and the paws of a giant puma or cougar, and had scales and spikes running along its body. These creatures were the amalgamation of several kinds of animals, and sometimes were even said to have feathers. The Potawatomi said they lived in the deepest part of the lake, and could upset the water and cause storms as they lashed their tails in fury. They were intelligent and could speak as well, with some tales telling of water panthers warning canoers that they were stealing from their lair. It was said that if you were foolish enough to paddle over top of where the beast was trying to slumber, the water would begin to roil around your boat. As you sat and tried to discern what was happening, a deep voice would bubble out of the water, warning you to turn back, lest you invoke the rage of the water panther. These panthers were usually considered malevolent and terrifying creatures. Their mortal enemies were the Thunderbirds, the *Chigwa* (pronounced Chig-yeah) who were the powerful protectors of the sky. Thunder was caused by the beatings of their wings and just their gaze could be deadly to humans.

There is a place on the water of Geneva Lake known as Conference Point, where the Potawatomi spoke of great battles between the Thunderbird and the Water Panther. The point is not named for a modern conference center, but instead for the meeting—the conference—of these great mythological beasts. The giant birds would throw eggs down at the water, striking like hailstones, while the panthers would lash out with high waves at their attackers. As the two mythological beasts locked in battle, the waves, wind, and thunder would grow to a fever pitch until massive thunderstorms would crash down on the shores of Lake Geneva.

To this day, strange thunderstorms do seem to pop up out of nowhere, catching swimmers and boaters unawares. Likely, the Potawatomi experienced these storms, and wove their tales to explain the seemingly inexplicable.

One of the most notorious modern day sightings of a massive bird attack happened in Lawndale, Illinois northeast of Springfield and about halfway between the site of Cahokia and Lake Geneva. On July 25, 1977 a few minutes after 8pm, right before dark, a seventy-pound ten-year-old named Marlon Lowe was playing outside with some friends when he was attacked by two gigantic birds who attempted to lift him off the ground like a falcon snatching up a mouse.

His mother Ruth Lowe came out to see him two feet in the air and fighting off black birds that she estimated had an eight-foot wingspan and claimed that they "were the biggest things I've ever seen."[17] One of the boy's punches finally made the winged beasts drop him from their talons, but left him terrified after a twenty foot ride. But it wasn't just her and Marlon who saw the birds, the other kids, her neighbor James Daniels, and his wife also admitted they'd seen the giant birds. And they were taken seriously by the local police who claimed they were probably turkey vultures, which can get an almost six foot wingspan, but Marlon and Ruth were convinced they were condors, which are the largest North American birds.

There was a story in a 1926 newspaper about a condor in Buenos Aires, Argentina snatching up a two-year old. But there's a similar story about a Scottish two-year old from the same year (remember we talked about how they would try to put tabloid news stories next to regular journalism?) So who knows the veracity of those tales. There's a similar tale in *The Milwaukee Sentinel* from 1910 about a bird that snatched a two-month old from her mother and took the child to a nearby nest. And while hunters used their sniper skills to kill the bird, by the time they got to the nest, the little girl was already dead.

With child-snatching birds being some kind of trendy fascination, there were more reports of giant birds stretching through central Illinois in the summer of 1977. Perhaps the Lowe's terrifying tale inspired the imaginations of nearby residents of the Land of Lincoln, but as we hear stories of the supernatural battles at Conference Point or as we admire the sacred mounds that have withstood the ravages of time, in their own way, the Mound Builders were documenting their own experience with these fantastic creatures.

---

[17] *The Dispatch*, Moline, Illinois, July 28, 1977

SPIRIT OF THE LAKE

While the indigenous people of the lake told stories of ancient elementals like the thunderbirds and the water panthers, they weren't the only ones to see unexplained things of supernatural origins. Some of these tales involve neither a ghost nor a beast in the waters, but something more ethereal.

In the *Chicago Tribune* in July 1899, a story ran about "Ghosts at Summer Resorts". Of course, Lake Geneva was mentioned, being that the city was the premier summer resort for anyone of substance from Chicago. The strange tale served as the cornerstone of the article. The *Tribune* tells the tale of four young people who had come for a respite from their "busy city to seek new inspiration in life from the green foliage, the singing birds, and the rippling waters." They went on a canoe trip one evening out on the water of Geneva Lake, and drifted onto a little cove far enough away from the lights of the hotels and the camps, so that all they could see were the lights of the stars above.

It was peaceful and wonderful, and they gazed at the sky and discussed the "mysteries of the twinkling stars" for hours. Their night was delightful, until they were shocked into attention by a brilliant white light. It was a steamer sweeping past them, nothing paranormal, and it caught them in its wake. The wash from the steamer was powerful enough to push the canoe onto the nearest beach, and there they sat for a minute until the ship passed them.

As they sat in their canoe on the beach, they attempted to gather themselves from what felt a bit like a near death experience. Nervous laughter and deep breaths were had, and then, one of the young men noticed a strange light emanating from underneath a nearby bush. He alerted his friends, and they all watched as it glowed brightly. They speculated at first that it might be "fox fire." Fox fire is an old fashioned term for an eerie phosphorescent light that radiates from certain types of fungus, and it makes decaying wood look like it's glowing in a downright supernatural way.

The greenish light slowly grew and spread as the men watched, and it stretched out towards their boat. As it did, they said it took the shape of a woman. This was plainly not fox fire. The mysterious woman was beautiful, yet they could see right through her as she materialized in front of them, glowing softly. A strange smell rose from the water, sharp and tangy, and the paper quoted them as feeling like they were "breathing the air of another sphere."

Scared but intrigued, one of the foursome stood up and challenged the phantasm, as his friends sat, frozen in abject horror.

"Who are you?" he cried, pointing at her. To their immense surprise, the spirit opened her mouth and answered in a soft, musical voice.

"I am the spirit of the lake," she said, "I was here at the beginning and I shall be here at the end. I wept when the red man departed, but I have learned to love his successor, the white. I know that the most turbulent of natures, the most proud and haughty who seek my shores, cannot altogether resist my influence. I shall always be here, but only to those whose hearts are open to the highest degree of love."

Talk about a loquacious spirit, and not exactly politically correct to boot. Most ghosts aren't quite as talkative as this spirit of the lake seems to be. Most often, when a spirit deigns to speak, it is nothing more than a moan, a groan, or even just a loud thumping knock from somewhere nearby. Rarely do spirits materialize and spout forth with a full soliloquy and philosophical musings!

It seems like a strange tale to put into the paper, but this story was nestled right next to a detailed haunting in Oconomowoc and a true crime in Michigan. The Mound Builders who lived in this place a thousand years ago did shape some of their mounds to represent the spirit of the water. Did that spirit approach these canoers in a non-threatening manner, with a beautiful and gentle face, so that they would understand and not feel the chill of fear? Does this spirit appear to others, and if so, in what form? Is she an indigenous legend, a lost spirit, or something else? Her origins and purpose are shrouded in mystery still, but the fact remains that she has been sighted, and she *does* have something to say, indeed.

JENNIE THE LAKE GENEVA SEA SERPENT

Do you know what a cryptid is?

A cryptid is a creature whose existence is suggested, but isn't quite proven. They are mysterious creatures that can't just quite seem to provide enough evidence to confirm that they exist. Famous cryptids include Bigfoot, Chupacabra, and the Moth Man. But that's not where the talk of cryptids ends, because the world *has* confirmed the existence of quite a few. Animals that we have in zoos today, like the giant squid, Komodo dragons, gorillas, manatees, and even the not so mystical duck-billed platypus were once claimed to be just as false as Bigfoot, but time proved them real. This confirmation is good news for Lake Geneva, because our clear lake waters are rumored to be home to a large monster!

Most active in "the narrows" part of the lake, which is nearly in the middle, where it only stretches a half a mile across, our sea serpent has quite a legacy. Folklorist Charles E. Brown wrote a pamphlet in the 1930s about the sea serpents of Wisconsin. Yes, you read that correctly—the sea serpents... of Wisconsin. Sea serpent sightings have been reported all around the state, including Rock Lake, Lake Mendota, Lake Michigan, and beyond. Brown referenced one particular creature in Geneva Lake that first started being sighted in the 1880s. The creature liked to overturn small boats, and sometimes people would see it in the wake of the big steamers that would cross the lake. Victims would report that the water would mysteriously boil up around them, and then their little boats would suddenly capsize.

Does that sound familiar? The boiling water, bubbling around vessels in the water? Perhaps the Potawatomi were not just telling tales, but really were reporting on actual happenings on the water.

It was in July of 1892, when a local man, Ed Fay, and his two sons were done fishing for the day when they saw a lizard-like head come up from the lake nearby their fishing boat. They described the creature as having sharp, pointy teeth, and an approximately ten foot long neck, covered in brown scales that were pale green on the bottom.

In September of 1902, the *Janesville Gazette* reported a snake-like beast some 65 feet long and 10 inches in diameter stalking the waves here. This time, they gave the creature its own nickname, "Jennie," potentially derived from the word "Geneva." Jennie was regarded as the terror of Geneva Lake.

The Milwaukee Sentinel added some details as well of this particular Jennie sighting. The article kept on calling the beast "his Snakeship" like you would call someone "your Lordship!" They, perhaps, did not wish to refer to the serpent by her first name, as that's just too familiar for a creature of that reported size. It is, after all, much more respectable to refer to anyone, even a lake monster, by the title she earned. The article talked about a Mrs. Buckingham of Sharon, Wisconsin, whose son was a Geneva Lake steamship captain. Out on the water with her son and a group of locals, she saw something strange emerge from the water. Realizing that it was a large creature, Mrs. Buckingham alerted everyone in her group to the beast, and a brave man by the name of Carl Henders even rowed out to try and confront the creature, but "His Snakeship" submerged and escaped. The group stared at the empty water, terrified and perplexed.

There were a few more reported sightings over the years, but as the Twentieth Century grew older, the tales of Jennie, the Geneva Lake Sea Serpent grew rarer and rarer. In our modern era, no one is reporting a mysterious snake-like creature of giant proportions. However, recent posts to local social media groups do show photos and reports of 8 to 12 feet long gar fish being both sighted in the shallows, and caught by industrious fishermen. Perhaps these creatures are the same species that were being sighted long ago? Or perhaps, something more insidious has been stalking the deep waters all along. At 142 feet deep, Geneva Lake is the second deepest lake in Wisconsin. There are plenty of places for Jennie, or any sort of large beast, to hide in the waters. If she did exist, and she died, there's plenty of places at the bottom of the lake where the body of "His Snakeship" might have landed and eventually eroded.

It's also possible that if she did exist, she chose to relocate, especially as modern times emerged with all of our noisy cars, music, and technology. Geneva Lake does empty into the White River, which empties into the Fox, which connects to the Illinois and finally the Mississippi. Could Jennie have just decided to move south in the Winter, like a cryptozoological snowbird?

Of course, as we mentioned before, Nineteenth Century newspapers had no ethical journalism issues with printing stories of ghosts and monsters so that they could sell more papers. So, of course we have to take everything with a grain of salt. But while improbable, it doesn't mean these stories are impossible. Cryptids are creatures that haven't been discovered yet. They could exist! These creatures don't defy the laws of physics, or necessarily have a supernatural component like a ghost, which requires a belief in a soul or spirit.

After all, it wasn't that long ago that someone saw a duck billed platypus for the very first time. As this person described the creature (that we now know full well is real and exists!), imagine how insane he must have seemed. He saw a furry creature with claws, a beaver tail, and a duck bill… laying eggs. As he explained it to his friend, one can only imagine that the friend offered to book him a one way ticket to a sanitarium in Lake Geneva for some of that famous "relaxation." And yet now, we know that these creatures are real and not at all supernatural.

So part of the fun of exploring these topics is leaving the door open for the possibility of things that we don't yet understand, otherwise we'll be the ones as foolish as those who once believed a creature like the platypus had to be a figment of someone's imagination.

THE DISPATCH

On July 7, 1895, a young family from Elgin, Illinois took to the waters of Geneva Lake for a day of relaxation and companionship. It was a hot, humid summer day, and the lake was incredibly crowded with other boaters, but that did not deter the Hogan family from making their way to the rental docks.

At nearly 3pm, John Hogan, a prominent doctor and director of the Elgin Sanitarium, chartered a small steamer named *The Dispatch*. The craft was beautiful, at nearly 40 feet long, and constructed out of oak boards, brass finishings, and plush interior upholstery. It boasted beautiful tapestry curtains that could be drawn around the seating area, as well. John's wife, Kittie, as well as their toddler son, boarded the boat, along with a few cousins from out of town.

Hugging the shoreline due to the crowded nature of the lake, the Hogan family enjoyed the beginnings of their day on the water, despite having much of their view obscured by the trees that overhang the lakeshore. Eventually, as the family and captain navigated towards Williams Bay at the opposite end of the lake, they began to notice that the sky was growing dark in the Southwest corner. They paid no heed, as no one else on the water seemed alarmed, as well. However, that would prove to be a poor decision indeed, as moments later, the heavy dark clouds raced in overhead, and it seemed as though the heavens themselves ripped open above the lake.

Torrential rain, high winds, and sharp hail pelted the water and surrounding areas. Mass chaos ensued, with boaters panicking to escape the lake and seek shelter. Reports would state later that a tornado had been sighted, dropping from the skies over the lake, and skimming along the water. Witnesses described a "great swath of foam" appearing along the lake where the storm touched it. The storm system in question would go on to cause damage and destruction all across the Midwest, and in Lake Geneva, over a thousand trees were reported as being downed. Numerous lakeside homes were damaged, as well. Thankfully, nearly everyone was able to abandon their crafts and rush to nearby homes and mansions to hide from the violent storm. Everyone, of course, except for the Hogan family.

Onlookers would later report that they observed *The Dispatch* veering back and forth in the water. The boat would speed along in one direction and then abruptly change course, with the tapestry curtains shut tight against the storm that raged outside. Back and forth it went, zigzagging in no meaningful way, until a large wave lifted up in front of it. When the water dropped back down, *The Dispatch* was nowhere to be seen, however some horrified witnesses along the shoreline reported seeing Kittie being tossed from the ship, clutching her child to her chest as the waves took them. Still others believed that they saw *The Dispatch* "plunge to the bottom."

After the storm ended, a few brave men boarded *The Majestic*, which was the largest steamer in the Geneva Lake fleet, and went out in search of the Hogan family. After combing the water, searching the shoreline, and looking anywhere they could, they came up empty handed. As *The Majestic* floated nearby the last known location of *The Dispatch*, however, finally one man looked down into the water adjacent to the steamer, and observed a dark shape floating just below the surface of the water.

The body of Kittie Hogan.

Detectives would later state in their records that they believed her "fashionable" dress helped hold her corpse afloat in the water. A fashionable dress in 1895 would have the Cinderella type sleeves—tight at the wrist to just above the elbow, and then a large circular pouf of fabric from elbow to shoulder. These sleeves are sometimes known as mutton chop sleeves. The detectives stated that those sleeves, along with the small purse she carried, appeared to have inflated with air as the was sucked under the water by the sinking of *The Dispatch*, and that small bit of air helped provide buoyancy to her body.

The team worked quickly and dove to the bottom of the lake, underneath where Mrs. Hogan floated. There, pinned by the 40 foot long oak boards that once made up the craft that carried him, was the body of Kittie's young son. His body was recovered quickly and brought aboard *The Majestic*. As the crew reached the surface, however, the body of Kittie was nowhere to be seen. They searched a bit longer, and came up empty handed. It was as though she appeared just to note the location of her son's body, and then vanished into thin air.

In the weeks that followed, the other members of the Hogan party and the captain would be located, their bodies washing up on various beaches and front lawns around Geneva Lake. Kittie's corpse would eventually be discovered, floating nearby where the initial tragedy took place.

It is, however, a bit of a local legend, that the "woman in white" commonly appears along the lakeshore, or even on the main decks of boats, just before a storm is about to strike the area. She's described as having a panic stricken look on her face. Sometimes, she's seen as nothing more than a quick flash of white light, as if lightning strikes nearby. Local lore is that this phenomenon is Kittie, coming back to warn us, so that we don't meet the same fate that her family did so very long ago.

Local legends also speak of a similar sight during storms. It is said that if you stand in the tower of the Black Pointe Estate, which looms high on a lakeshore hill nearby where *The Dispatch* sank, lightning strikes will illuminate a small white shape in the water. Some say that it is the white dressing gown of the Hogan baby, and that he can be seen disappearing into the waves, over and over, stuck on repeat. Still others say that if you gaze up at Black Pointe during a storm, you might see the outline of terrified spirits standing in the tower, watching the water in abject horror, reliving the most frightening moments that they experienced during their lives.

Whatever happened that day, and whatever has happened since, it is a comforting thought, at least, that the Hogan family, despite being torn apart tragically during that fateful storm, is reunited once more in the afterlife.

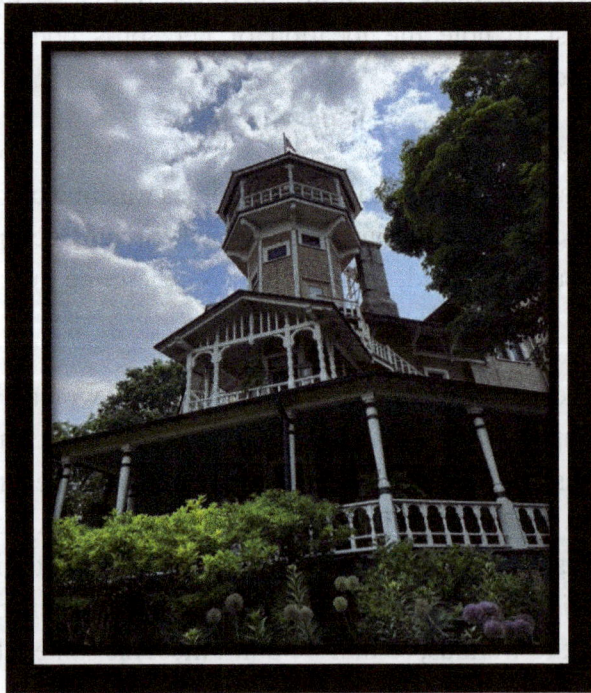

18 Black Point Estate. Photo: Rita Mae Moore

ELM PARK

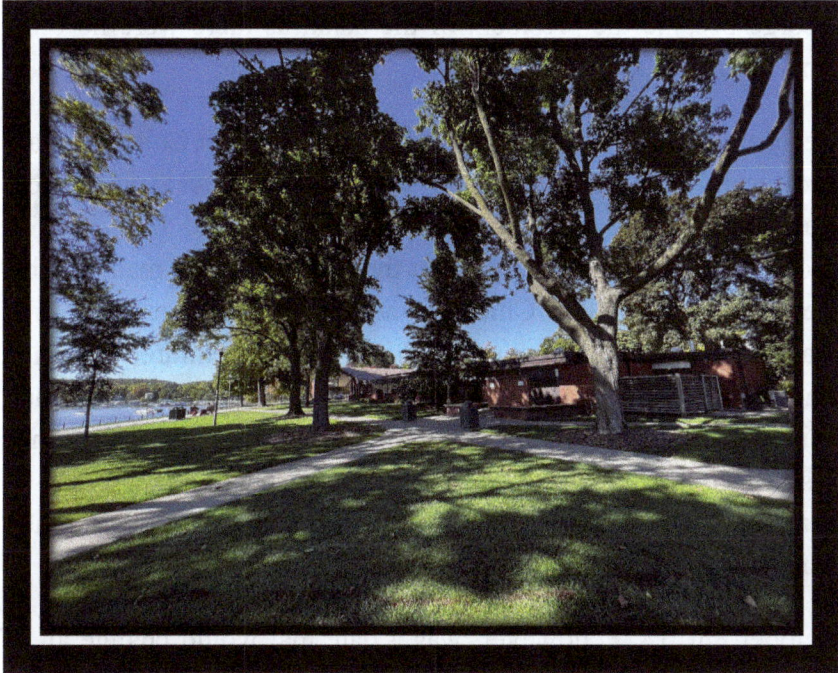

19

When walking around and enjoying Lake Geneva, you'll be sure to find yourself in Elm Park, right by the Lake Geneva Public Library. Locals even call the park "Library Park." The park itself is adjacent to the Riviera Beach, right on the edge of the west side of the downtown blocks. Elm Park was gifted, so to speak, to the city by the Sturges family in 1894.

The Sturges family's history is synonymous with the history of Lake Geneva, and like many early families in the area, the Sturges family

---

[19] Elm Park, also known as Library Park, and Lake Geneva Public Library.
Photo: Rita Mae Moore

started their rise to wealth in Chicago. In the 1860s, George Sturges worked at Northwestern National Bank in Chicago. He was the son of Solomon Sturges, one of Chicago's early business leaders. To show you how small the bank was back then, according to Alfred Andreas' *History of Chicago Volume 3*, George was the cashier at the bank until his brother Stephen retired. When Stephen retired, George became the president of the bank, as there were no other employees.

George met and married Mary Delafield in 1862 in Chicago. Mary had recently moved to Chicago with her family, relocating from Kansas. It was love at first sight for George and Mary, by all accounts. The new couple lived at the Sturges family mansion that George's father built in Chicago, and over the first decade of their marriage, George and Mary would have eight children together. They vacationed in Lake Geneva every summer, bringing their children up to splash in the waves and dig in the sand. They owned a small cottage nearby Elm Park. They'd spend a few weeks in Wisconsin, enjoying the late summer, and then back down to their main home in Chicago for the winter.

October 8th, 1871, however, was a date that would change all of that. The evening of October 8th, citizens in Chicago began to notice a reddish glow in the sky, followed by the unmistakable smell of smoke in the air. A fire began to burn in Chicago that would end up decimating a third of the city and taking hundreds of lives. The Great Chicago Fire, as it came to be known, changed the landscape and history of the Midwest. The Sturges family mansion was one of the homes destroyed in the fire. Thankfully, the family was uninjured.

The Sturges family, like so many other wealthy Chicagoans who survived the inferno, were forced to relocate to their summer homes in Lake Geneva. The population of the once small Wisconsin town grew rapidly towards the end of 1871, thanks to the fire. As these families relocated, they brought with them their employees, staff, and businesses, which required more homes to be built in the Geneva Lake area. The history and growth of Lake Geneva is directly linked to the tragedy of the Great Chicago Fire.

George and Mary brought their family to the small cottage, and realizing quickly that their large family wasn't going to be comfortable in the property as it stood, they also purchased the five surrounding properties. The goal? To not have nearby neighbors as they built their dream home. They and their eight children lived in the little house for a few years, while they built their proper mansion. When it was completed, they named it Snug Harbor, which was finished in 1881. Snug Harbor was a unique name, given that the mansion was incredibly large.

The Sturges family was a bit eccentric, by Victorian standards. Their parlor featured such a size that they had large furniture custom made to fill it. Once completed, the furniture was so large that anyone who sat upon it looked like a small child, even adults! Snug Harbor stood just outside of the proper city limits, along what is now called Snake Road. Those grounds are now known as Covenant Harbor, which is a local youth camp.

George passed away in 1890 at the relatively young age of 52. He left Mary in charge of all of his estate, which was incredibly rare for the time. In the Victorian Era, property and wealth normally went down to the first born son, with widows left to wear the ubiquitous mourning attire, forced to live in a spare room belonging to some other family member. After 10 years of mourning, a widow could add a single piece of silver jewelry, and after 20 years, if they were still alive, they could upgrade to gold. For George to will everything to Mary and not his son was unique and pretty much unheard of. Women were seen more as property than person, so for her to become a standalone, wealthy citizen was a rare occurrence indeed.

Mary did great things with the money and clout she inherited. She donated almost everything back to Lake Geneva, financing many art installations, a beautiful pipe organ at an Episcopalian church on Broad Street, and conserving land for public park access. In 1894, she donated the property where her original cottage stood, which would come to be known as Elm Park to the city of Lake Geneva, with the stipulation that it be used as a library and a public park. She didn't want only the wealthiest citizens to be able to enjoy the lake. Mary wanted everyone to have a chance to relax and play, just as her family had, regardless of class or income. Not only that, but in a proto-feminist move, she also made a stipulation that the board of the library that would be built would be comprised of a female majority. Since 1894, the Lake Geneva Public Library has been run and staffed almost entirely by women. What an incredible legacy!

Mary donated much to the city of Lake Geneva, helping create churches, the YMCA, the library, and more. A hall at the prestigious Field Museum in Chicago also bears her name, honoring her for her contributions there, as well. Her name is carved on the side of the beautiful "Three Graces" statue and fountain that stands at the tip of Flat Iron Park in Lake Geneva. The statue bears the name of ten fascinating, powerful women from early Lake Geneva history, and was erected in 1916 with the words "In Memory of Good Friends" etched into the third side.

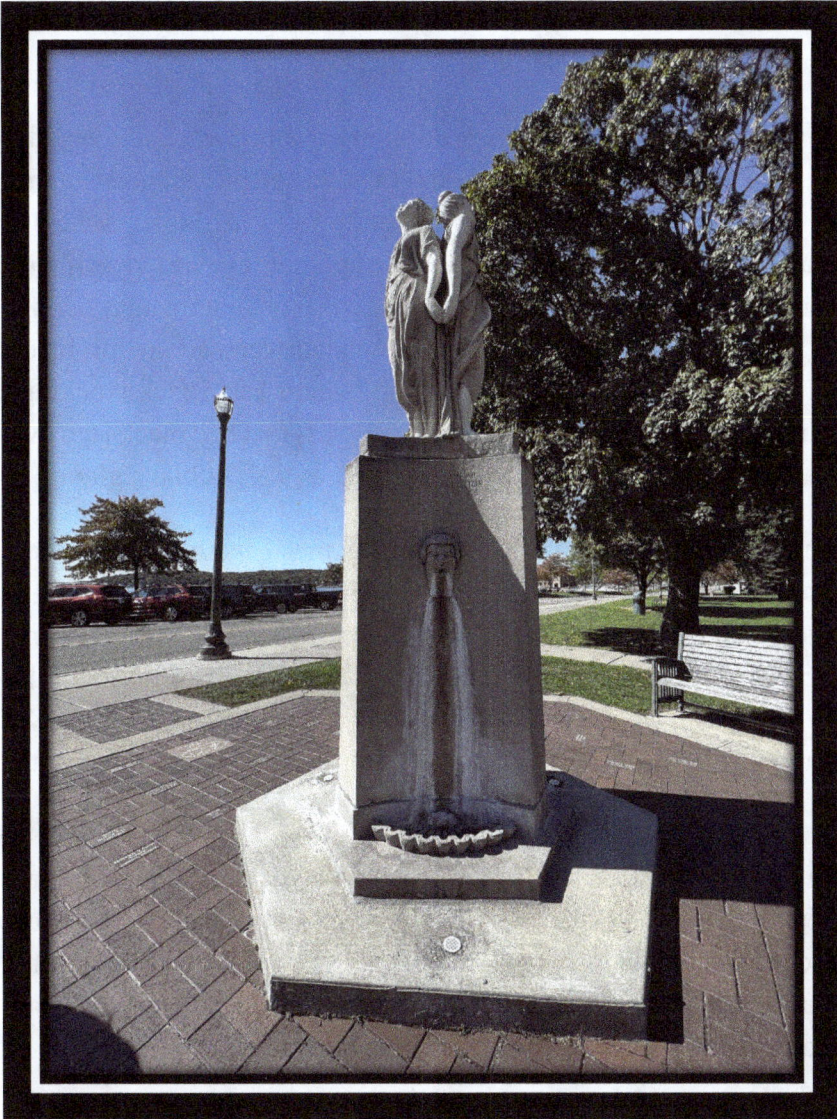

20

While the Sturges family was famous around the turn of the 20th Century, unless you're a student of history, you might not be aware

---

[20] Three Graces statue in Flat Iron Park, Bearing the name Mary Sturges as well as other notable women. Photo: Rita Mae Moore

of them. So, it makes it even more interesting when an eyewitness had an unusual encounter in this very park.

A woman and her husband were visiting from Chicago and decided to have a picnic. As they were having their picnic, the husband sat at the base of the tree, and his wife sat down facing him. As she was reaching to get him a soda, she noticed that his eye had grown wide and his face turned white. He pointed to something behind her and as she turned around, she saw a woman dressed in all black, nineteenth century clothing standing behind her. Black stockings, black lace up boots, and a long sleeved dress that had black lace over it. In addition, she wore a wide black hat as well as black gloves.

The first thing the woman thought was that, why is she wearing these clothes, it's eighty degrees outside! Is there some kind of festival or historical thing going on? She turned around to her husband, wondering why he was so terrified, and found him sitting with his mouth agape. Deciding that her spouse was useless in her endeavor for knowledge, she turned back around and decided to ask the woman in black what she wanted.

She was stunned, as she turned around, to find herself nose to nose with the strange woman. As they sat, eyes locked mere inches from each other, the woman's mouth opened, as if she intended to speak. Yet her lips did not seem to move, although a sound could be heard that was more air and wind than voice.

The next thing the woman remembers is that she was standing on the other side of the park, a good quarter mile away, with no idea as to how she got there. She was alone, and very confused. It was as if she was in a trance that suddenly lifted. She ran back to find her husband sitting under the tree, seemingly fine. Asking her husband what happened, he said that she had walked away with a "green lady" and he, still frightened by the woman who had appeared out of thin air, moved to stand up, too. He asked if he should come along, but the unknown woman shook her head and motioned for him to sit back down. He described the woman linking arms with his wife, and the two of them walked away, talking to each other and giggling like schoolgirls. She had no memory of what they discussed or why, or even of walking away with the stranger.

Other people have reported seeing this woman in Nineteenth Century clothing in the park all the way back to the 1970s. Some people have said she'll follow you as you walk around the park. She often seems to fall into step with groups of women, and often declines to speak to or walk with men if they approach her.

A few years after American Ghost Walks started in Lake Geneva, a guest on the tour had quite a revelation. As the guide, Rita, explained the tale of the woman in black, one crowd member seemed increasingly uneasy, even beyond the normal shivers that travel down spines. When the story ended, the woman stepped forward and explained that she had seen the mysterious woman in black herself some years back. In the mid-nineties, the guest had been a high school student attending Prom at the Riviera, which is adjacent to Elm Park. She described sneaking out of the dance with her date and a few friends. The group went down onto the beach, and were splashing and playing in the water. Next thing she remembered, she was walking along the far edge of the beach, alone, with no memory of what had happened. About forty five minutes had passed that she had no recollection of. She went back into the dance, where her friends all informed her that they had thought that her mother had picked her up early. She asked what they meant.

"Wasn't your mom the lady in a black dress that was staring at us down on the beach?" they asked. "We thought you were in trouble for sneaking out of the dance!"

The tour guest went on to explain that for decades, she had no idea that it was anything paranormal...until she heard the tales of the sightings of the woman in black on the tour. That was when she knew that she had truly been contacted by a spirit that night.

Could this be Mary Delafield Sturges checking in on her beloved lakefront property and the library that she bequeathed to the city of Lake Geneva? Does she have a message of empowerment for the women who are using the park now? Or is it a warning? The people who have seen her say they don't feel frightened, so we'd like to think that Mary is just still making sure that the common folk get to enjoy the lake, just like she intended in 1894.

SNAKE ROAD

21

Of a less outwardly haunted nature, but still very much worth mentioning in any book covering the fascinating sites and sights in Lake Geneva, is Snake Road. Any visitor to town should make a point of driving down the rustic road, for the history as much as the beauty.

To find Snake Road, take highway 50, also known as Main Street, to the West, heading out of town. After driving up a hill, and just as the highway branches into a divided highway, there will be a sign

---

21 Motorcyclists enjoying fall colors on Snake Rd. Photo credit: Signalfire. Motorcyclists: Joshua and Rita Mae Moore.

for a rustic road on the left, South side of the road. It's not clearly marked with the name Snake Road, but a sign for Covenant Harbor is visible.

The road itself is a narrow, winding, two lane road, hence the name, snake. What makes this short drive so unique is that it serves as the main access to all of the mansions that sit on the north shore of the lake. When the leaves drop, the homes themselves can be viewed, with their own winding driveways and beautiful landscaping. Autumn is a particularly beautiful time to visit, with the foliage erupting into bright colors in every direction (just watch out for photographers and tourists standing in the middle of the road to capture that perfect image!)

Sights of note include the Wrigley property, of Wrigley Gum fame, with the crossed fencing on both sides of the road. Further down, the former Driehaus estate sits, also known as Glanworth Gardens, formerly Wadsworth Hall, not visible from the road except for the spectacular entry gate. The gate, with red bricks and beautiful landscaping, boasts cement lion heads that once stood in Central Park, and the landscaping was created by the famed Frederick Olmstead, who also created Central Park and the Biltmore Estate grounds.

Driving down Snake Road, you'll pass the former homes of families with names like Wacker, Selfridge, Wrigley, Sears, and more. Even more exciting, many of these homes served as meeting points for the suffragette movement of the early 1900s. This 2.5 mile road is not to be missed.

22

Nearly every building that stands in the downtown area of Lake Geneva is registered as a historic place, with several blocks of downtown having been approved on the National Historic Registry. Not only is this an excellent pedigree, but also, with old historic places, there are always legends. People talk in Lake Geneva about boarded off tunnels underneath the downtown, connecting all the buildings and going out near the lake. Many of the mansions that ring the lakeshore also are home to numerous underground tunnels, running down to the water and beyond. It's often rumored that they were getaway tunnels used by gangsters during Prohibition. When the law comes knocking at the Speakeasy door, it was a much safer escape than trying to get out through the building.

The truth of the tunnels is slightly less salacious, even though the tunnels did exist. In truth, instead of running rum or hiding women, booze, money, or anything else that was forbidden during prohibition, these tunnels served more as cold storage. The lakeside tunnels often supported the ice harvesting businesses on the lakeshore, and of course, it was easier to traverse long distances on foot underground, especially during the winter.

All over Wisconsin you hear stories of gangsters, especially one in particular. Who has not heard of Al Capone coming for a visit, passing through, or spending the night at a nearby inn? In fact, it feels like Al Capone didn't spend a second of the 1920s Prohibition Era in Chicago! There might be some truth to a few of the rumors, particularly in the Geneva Lakes area. Lake Como, northwest of Geneva Lake, is often reputed to have been the more popular gangster spot, due to it being much more secluded and private. To this day, businesses such as the French Country Inn on the shores of Lake Como boast bullet holes that are still in their walls, remnants of long ago mafia shootouts. Lake Geneva, however, has nothing so concrete to prove the visitations of the mafia. If they were in the city itself, they either minded their business, or, more likely, they avoided the more populated area. There's no doubt that gangsters did pass through the area, with the Northwoods of Wisconsin being a popular site for hideaways and vacation homes from the Chicago mafia. Lake Geneva stands directly in between those two destinations, and who cannot resist a stop in such a beautiful spot?

The building at 731 W. Main St was built not by a criminal, but indeed by one of the pillars of Lake Geneva's early days, Frank Sherman Moore. Frank came to Lake Geneva in 1871 (as did many other notable names, forced out of Chicago thanks to the blaze that burned in October), and started working at the hardware business that was already established on Main Street. But Frank was a hard worker and an entrepreneurial spirit himself, and by 1890, he took the business over. In 1903, Frank updated the building. The front was covered in Bedford Limestone, which can still be seen on the second floor, and there were even columns in the front to make it a classically beautiful structure. Above the columns was a stone header and in it was carved, "Paints Tinware F.S. Moore Hardware." That header is still visible to this day.

When Frank passed away on November 10th, 1936, 731 West Main Street remained a hardware store for decades after his death. While there were new owners, the business was still called Moore Hardware, in his honor. Frank himself left a huge mark on Lake Geneva. He was elected the mayor of Lake Geneva in 1898, and served as postmaster throughout the first decade of the Twentieth Century. Frank was also a founding member of the Lake Geneva Knights of Pythias. Now, as compelling as it would be to say that the Knights of Pythias was some secret society on par with the Freemasons for diabolical conspiracies secretly in charge of the world, it's actually a respectable charity organization. Famous Pythians do include Presidents Warren G. Harding, William McKinley, and Franklin Delano Roosevelt, as well as jazz legend Louis Armstrong and Vice President Hubert Humphrey. However, the most nefarious thing about the organization we could find was that you weren't supposed to drink alcohol as a member. Which in the time of Prohibition, was expected of many local leaders.

Now about the limestone. Why is that important? Remember the earlier story about Havenwood and the old Oakwood Springs Sanitarium? The "Stone Tape Theory" was referenced—the theory that hauntings are just leftover traumatic energy, and can be recorded into the natural structure like grooves on a vinyl album. It's true that limestone buildings often have more haunted stories than others. One theory about why limestone is more paranormally sensitive is from paranormal researcher Timothy Yohe. One of Yohe's ideas is that, since limestone is made up of former organic matter, it might contain some residual living energy that spirits might be able to tap into. Because it's calcified bodies of sea life, he refers to it as "paranormal plankton." This stone that is created out of compacted, former organic matter becomes a sponge. Like attracts like, and the energy of the potential haunt is more easily absorbed and stored in these stones.

Now, before the present business at the location, it was a shop known as Bouquets, and there was an active presence that the employees often felt. They felt it was a feminine presence and nicknamed the spirit "Jennifer." Jennifer loved to cause mischief around the store, especially focusing on customers who were rude, or those that she simply didn't seem to like. Jennifer even almost made a lamp fall on a complaining customer one time. Generally, the young spirit would just move around candles, turn lights on and off, and make little noises when no one else could have made them. Jennifer is what is commonly referred to as a poltergeist. Not referencing the terrifying movie, but instead, poltergeist is the German word for a "noisy ghost," and usually describes an entity that likes to make mischief, just as Jennifer does.

However, the only physical manifestation inside the building that was seen was a male looking phantom. This man was seen on a security camera, with broad grayish shoulders. The women who have seen him all agree that he did not feel threatening, but instead, comforting, as though a father figure had materialized to keep them safe and protected. As these employees were closing up the business at night, counting down the till and flipping off light switches, they reported seeing him appear, as if he was standing watch over them. He's often seen in the front window of the store, watching for any potential disturbance to those within. Who knows who that was? Could it have been a gangster? An old employee? Could it be Frank Moore himself revisiting the place where he spent much of his life? In life, he was described as being a kind, protective man, and the women who report seeing the phantom describe him in exactly the same way.

Either way, you can still see the entrance to the famous tunnels underneath the building in the downstairs of the store, and one of the employees in the mid 2000s did unearth an extremely old gambling ledger full of numbers, hanging on a nail just inside the tunnel entrance. Well, maybe Al Capone did visit Lake Geneva after all!

However, on a visit there in 2017 while working out the route for our ghost tour, we ended up having our own experience at the shop, which is now a fairly unassuming shop full of designer plates, vases, soaps, and other types of home wares. The group was the owner of the company and two of our tour guides, one of whom, Rita (co-author of this book) had worked there when it was Bouquets. So we thought it might be good to go in there and see if we could get any new stories.

It was a sunny Spring afternoon before the tourist season had begun and when we entered the store was empty besides the friendly owner. She appeared to be in her forties, with auburn hair running to her shoulders, and she had a friendly smile for us. When we inquired about any kinds of paranormal activity in the store, she smiled and said nothing like that has ever happened to her and since she's Catholic she doesn't believe in that kind of stuff. Okay, well, at least she didn't kick us out!

Rita mentioned her previous employment in the building and that she was familiar with the store and asked the owner if we could take a look around in the basement. Since there was no one else in the place, the sweet lady said that's completely fine and offered to take us down there. We went down the stairs cheerfully and the lady was being perfectly lovely about everything.

We were laughing and joking a bit as we took in the surroundings of the basement. Nothing seemed too spooky, after all, it was the middle of a beautiful day outside. It wasn't too musty and it had a regular cement floor, so not like a creepy crypt or anything. Random items from the store filled the shelves and were placed strategically across the ground. There were no basement windows or anything, so the light came from a few bulbs with pull chains, but it wasn't too dark or dim or particularly eerie. It was a normal basement and while we might have been hoping that Ghost Jennifer would come jumping out at us from a hidden corner, she was nowhere to be found. The walls are old and of course, it feels like it's been around for a century, but that's pretty standard for the area. All in all, a regular old basement with some nooks and crannies. There was a semi-crumbled entrance to what looks like it could have been an underground tunnel system, but it seemed to have been filled in, which makes sense because that could be a flooding nightmare. But that at least fuels the imagination for what could be a gangster rum-running story for the tour.

Our former employee/tour guide showed us where she found the gambling notebook as we crossed the floor. As we got to a slightly less well-lit area, it seemed like the basement went on for a while in the dark. We came upon a section where there were some studs up for a side storage area where it seemed like walls were never put up, or the walls had been taken down. Either way, there was nothing too exciting about the slightly unfinished construction of a storage area. Not strange because it was probably on the to-do list of the owners as something to get around to eventually.

As we were walking, the lady from the store was talking happily. "Here's where we keep the extra inventory and I've been down here alone plenty of times. I've never seen or felt anything...." And her voice trailed off as we got closer to the unfinished storage area. She was trailing slightly behind the group and because she suddenly stopped talking, we all turned around to her. Her eyes were watering and she continued weakly, "There's just something about this corner, I just.." And she stopped again. Her eyes teared up more heavily and she started crying in front of us, openly. Real weeping. She was completely overcome with emotion.

Our other tour guide said, "It's the little girl, isn't it?" She continued, "You lost someone like the little girl. The little girl that's still here, in that room over there, in the corner." She pointed to the unfinished storage area. "That's why she's reaching out to you." The woman weakly nodded through her tears. There was an intense energy in the room, a palpable static electricity. Something had just happened and it felt like the weather in the basement had changed. The woman embraced the guide in a kind of hug and turned around and walked back towards the stairs.

To normal eyes, it was just a corner and an unfinished storage closet. But the air was sucked out of the room witnessing this woman who doesn't believe in ghosts and had previously steadfastly insisted that she had zero paranormal experiences in this place *except* when we got to the corner of the basement that makes her sob inexplicable.

A little stunned, we walked back to the stairs slowly and you could hear some people chatting. Instead of just us eccentrics, there were actual customers in the store. The woman wiped her eyes, steadied herself, put on her best smile, and got back upstairs to talk to them and hopefully make a sale. We thanked her for her time, she nodded, got to the real customers, and we walked out into the sunlight.

The guide who had comforted the owner then mentioned that she's "sensitive" and she detected the presence of a little girl who was in that corner. It wasn't the lady's little girl, but the spirit was attracted to the shopkeeper because she had lost a child close to her. Who's the girl in the basement? Is that Jennifer? Is she someone connected to the building or a presence that wandered in? We don't have the answers and that experience just created more questions.

GENEVA TAP HOUSE

While construction began in 1926, the Geneva Theater officially opened its doors in 1928. The grand opening was a huge event, with the theater being a cutting edge property and a massive draw to the small midwestern town, even the Governor of Wisconsin, Fred Zimmerman, attended to celebrate.

The theater was designed in a Mediterranean Revival style, and like most theaters built in the 1920s, it not only was built to show movies, but was home to live vaudeville performances as well. There was an orchestra that could play along with the show, and as technology advanced, a retractable silver screen was installed. Imagine the mind blowing feeling as, after a performance ended, the screen rolled out to show a film reel, and then, when finished, slid to the side to reveal dancers poised to perform! Indeed, the *Janesville Gazette* has claimed that none other than the world famous Marx Brothers performed on stage in the theater's heyday. Other notable performers include the original movie Dracula, Bela Lugosi, and the down-home humorist, Will Rogers. These names serve as proof that the theater was a crown jewel in the Midwest.

The original stage with the balcony and orchestra pit was intact, and was in place until there was an addition put on the north side of the building in 1975. Other changes in the 70s included splitting off the balcony and splitting the addition into four separate theaters. Money had already become scarce for the theater, and they hoped that the ability to show multiple features would help. It did not.

Unfortunately, the Geneva Theater fell into some disrepair for most of the 90s. In the early 2020s, the theater had been revamped under new ownership and tried to start thriving again as a cinema and performance space. However, that wouldn't last long, and in 2022, the space reopened, reimagined as a self-serve tap house boasting fifty different types of beer to try.

But as with a lot of the different venues that we've investigated, there's just something about old theaters that seem to make these kinds of buildings more haunted than others, and stories persist of strange activity on the site.

Whether it's all the blood, sweat, and tears that actors put into productions, or the laughter, sadness, and all the emotions that art can elicit in an audience, theaters seem to be just the ideal places to replay those hauntings that seem to get embedded in the walls of a place. Or maybe just these actors and actresses are hams who can't even let death keep them from hogging any spotlight that they can get.

Think, truly, of the theory of the stone tape hauntings. The theory goes that energy, particularly from intense emotional moments, becomes stored in the natural elements around us. That energy is released over time, repeating a sound or movement like a record on a record player. What is an excellent performance, if not energy? An actress stands on stage, night after night, weeping and pouring her soul into a role. And the audience, feeling her performance, weep in their seats. That energy is real, and it washes over the walls of the theater over, and over, and over again. How could a theater not be haunted with that kind of energetic build up over time?

There's at least two ghosts in this theater that have decided to stick around even after their final curtain call on Earth. One of the presences that people feel is thought of as a male. It's a louder, more boisterous ghost, and when he decides to make his presence known people will smell smoke in the theater as well as hearing footsteps and bumps in the dark. Numerous tour guests, over the years, have inexplicably smelled cigar smoke at this site. Employees of the theater, going even back into the nineties, believe that this spirit is a former manager that likes to make sure that the staff, even today, is working hard. They reported that he would stomp down the corridors and linger, an opposing presence just behind them, the smell of cigar smoke curling into their nostrils. When they turn, there's no one there.

But there is also an apparition of a female who has been seen on several occasions. Now, while the revamped theater was going to carry on the tradition of live performances, one of the more detailed stories comes from a woman who was trying to do a performance in the theater before the renovation. She was going to be performing with her boyfriend, and as they were getting the tour of the premises, they started getting an intensely unpleasant feeling. As they stood on the stage, they heard a strange loud thump coming from the stairs off to the side of stage left. When they asked the owner if they could go check it out, she agreed, telling them that the only thing in that direction was the old dressing rooms that used to be functional back in the 30s.

As the woman and her boyfriend walked towards the old dressing room, they felt strongly that they were walking into a sudden cold spot. Not necessarily supernatural of course, but a common occurrence during ghostly encounters. Perhaps you've felt something similar, where the hair on your neck rises just as your stomach drops with the sudden chill. The theory behind cold spots is that an entity needs to gather energy to make contact, to make a noise, or just to do whatever spooky thing it has its sights set on. The entity will gather up energy from around itself, much like someone gathering up a sheet off of a bed. We, in our human bodies, stumble into that lack-of-energy spot, and we sense it as cold (and frightening), because we do not have anything else to reference it with. But, on our most primal level, we sense it as dangerous, and our desire to flee is activated. How many times have you gotten a chill coming up the basement stairs, and perhaps you ran quickly up the final few steps?

She described the feeling of stumbling through the cold spot in the theater thusly, "like the air was dead or something." They heard the sound of a woman laughing in the distance, and began to follow it, but as they did, the laughter seemed to get farther and farther away. She continually walked in and out of the cold spots of "dead air." As the activity continued, they began to become increasingly frightened, and after having had enough, they decided to walk back up to the stage. As her boyfriend went to collect their belongings from behind the curtain, the woman turned around and saw exactly who was laughing. It was a female form in her late 20s, who looked to be in costume, as if she was getting ready for her stage entrance. As the witness stared at the ghost, she said that she just felt a great sadness, as though heartache and tragedy was emanating off of the entity.

Then without warning, the apparition vanished.

Now, the couple who encountered the phantom actress have also heard since that it is the ghost of a woman who committed suicide by leaping from the balcony of the theater. This tale, of the suicidal, heartbroken actress, permeates Lake Geneva. However, we couldn't find any historical reports to back that up, but we've certainly heard from multiple witnesses that they have seen the actress themselves. Sometimes she's standing on the stage, sometimes sitting in one of the seats, staring up at the stage. Either way, any time she appears, she doesn't just exit stage left, she pulls off a much more impressive feat by completely vanishing before the eyes of the stunned witnesses who had just seen a ghost, when all they paid for was a movie.

PHANTOM PHONE CALLS

On your very worst day, when you need help and safety, 911 is there, ready to help. A simple push of the buttons can bring police, fire, rescue, and a myriad of other services to you for whatever assistance is needed. It seems, however, that mere mortals are not the only ones calling the emergency line, at least in Lake Geneva.

In the mid 2010s, in the middle of a dark and stormy night, the 911 line rang inside of the Lake Geneva Police Department. The dispatcher at the time answered, as she usually did, and immediately heard dead air. This is called a "911 open line," and most of the time, it's unintentionally caused by someone bumping their phone. The protocol is the same—check the number against computer records in the police department, while simultaneously calling it back to see if someone answers. When the call comes in, it drops a bullseye graphic on a computer map to show where the call likely was located, and an officer needs to be dispatched to that location to see if there are any people in need of assistance.

The dispatcher did exactly that, noting that the call was from a landline located in a residence along South Lakeshore Drive. That was good, as landlines, as rare as they are nowadays, are infinitely simpler to trace and locate, making the call much easier to handle. She dispatched an officer, and a second offered to go along, being that it was quite dark and rainy. The dispatcher attempted to call the number back, and was met with a busy signal. She relayed the information to the officers, and waited patiently for their report back.

Time ticked by slowly, and there was no word from her coworkers. After about 10 minutes, the dispatcher grew worried that something had happened, so she radioed the team, asking for a status check. After a long pause, one replied.

"Um," the officer said, a nervous giggle caught in her throat, "what was the address again?" The dispatcher responded with the information, and after another long pause, the officer's voice cut through the air over the radio. "Yeah, there's no house here."

Dispatch rapidly double checked her information, but it was all accurate. The officers cleared the call, and came straight back to the police department. Arriving in the dispatch room, they both looked visibly confused (and very wet from the rain).

The officers went on to explain that the address had been correct, and that there had been a house there just a day or two prior. But when they arrived to check for any emergencies, instead, they were met with an empty construction site. The entire building, including the foundation, had been torn down and cleared away, leaving nothing more than a muddy hole in the ground. The dispatcher was perplexed.

In order to get a busy signal on a phone you're calling, there must *actually* be a phone somewhere. A disconnected line would not give a busy signal, nor could a leftover, severed wire from a torn down house cause a phone to ring. To confirm, the dispatcher had neighboring agencies check their records for the name associated with the number and the home, and even called the phone company to double check that service had been shut off to that site, and that it wasn't possible for telephone wire remnants to make calls on its own.

It's often said that construction is like shaking a paranormal bird cage, causing spirits and leftover energy to become riled up and more active than usual. It seems as though that evening, a confused spirit may have called for help, perhaps upset over the destruction of the home and property in which he lingered.

That's not the only time that 911 has rang due to phantom purposes. In 2018, a restaurant located along the lakeshore in downtown Lake Geneva, currently known as Oakfire, called 911 at about 3am. The caller on the line was completely terrified, whispering in a panic into the receiver. She explained that the staff had been cleaning up for the night, after the business was closed and locked, when suddenly, loud crashing started to happen within the building. The few employees couldn't easily see what caused the banging, and ran into the basement. Once underground the banging and crashing reached a fever pitch, sounding like a hurricane was tearing the place apart. The caller was in tears, begging for help, positive that some drunk patron had broken in and was destroying the property.

Officers were dispatched, and given the violent sounds of the call, multiple squads arrived, lights and sirens blaring. Upon their arrival, the business was silent, with no movement inside. The officers checked the perimeter and then moved inside, checking everywhere for whomever had been causing the ruckus.

The property was completely empty, save for the terrified waiters that had barricaded themselves in the basement, and not a single item was out of place in the restaurant itself. The employees were visibly shaken and frightened as the officers brought them out of the basement, completely confused as to how they had experienced something so intense that seemed to have never happened at all.

The officers cleared the call, returning to their late night patrol duties, just as perplexed.

GENEVA LAKE MUSEUM

At the Geneva Lake Museum, you can travel back in time, through the decades of the town's history. There's a Main Street that starts in the time of Chief Big Foot and ends in the late Twentieth Century. You can see exhibits that discuss the World's Fair buildings that were brought over from Chicago and rebuilt on site, such as the Idaho Exhibition.

The Idaho Exhibition of 1893 was a building that created a great stir at the World's Fair, because it was made of millions of logs from Idaho's state forests and basaltic lava rocks. After the fair was done, a Mrs. Celia Wallace bought the building and reconstructed it in Lake Geneva. She was going to make it a home for troubled boys, but the site they chose to rebuild it in ended up being a bog, and the mosquitoes proved to be too much. Wallace abandoned the building, and eventually traded it to a local contractor for a pearl. The contractor thought he might fix it up and sell it, but it didn't work out for him, either.

There was trouble starting on the second day of construction, when a great storm hit the town, causing delay and destruction. Then a few weeks later, a group of boys was throwing rocks at the windows of the building when they unexpectedly heard horses' hooves and a piercing scream; yet no horses or riders were present. Thomas Verhin, of Niles Center, Illinois, reported seeing a cowboy on a bucking bronco bursting out of one of the doors of the building as the boys stood in front, transfixed by confusion and fear. He is quoted in a 1902 edition of the *Chicago Inter Ocean*, saying that "the worst part of the business was that the cowboy wasn't real, and neither was the bronco. They were both ghosts, just as sure as I'm alive. I didn't stop to see whether the spirit horse would collide with me. I ran… as hard as I could go, yelling at every bound."

The house that was so meticulously rebuilt was already reduced to decay by 1902. The theory, according to the newspaper writers who were quoting "those who pretend to know anything about ghosts," was that proud Idaho pioneers were haunting the building, because they were upset that it was in such disrepair, and were angered by the usage of valuable, historical wood and rock for unnecessary purposes.

Also at the Geneva Lake Museum is an exhibit about Northwestern Military Academy, a building deemed so spooky that it was good enough for shooting scenes for *Damien: The Omen 2* in the late 70s. Boys who studied and lived at the military academy even got to be in the film, appearing as background extras. We talked with the daughter of the former headmaster, and she described growing up in Davidson Hall, the main building that was torn down a few years ago after the academy merged campuses with another Southeastern Wisconsin school. She said that, while it could be an eerie old building, she never had any experiences there, but that doesn't mean the boys weren't superstitious. She explained that the boys would claim that they saw the ghost of school founder Harlan Page Davidson roaming the halls. One former teacher describes his students telling him that something was pulling the blankets off of their beds while they slept, opening the windows, and throwing their textbooks in the garbage. His students wondered aloud if it could be the ghosts of old students who died in the First or Second World Wars and then were buried on the site. One former seventh grader, in the 1980s, even wrote about his experience at the academy, saying, "I am now 33 years old and I can honestly tell you that I am still bothered by some of the things that happened in that place…. There were so many ghosts there… I heard they tore that place down and all I can say is that I am glad."

CEMETERIES

Lake Geneva is home to a number of cemeteries, beautiful and full of history. While there are no known specters that wander the burial grounds, there have been some reports of strange lights floating through one cemetery, and other homes nearby another cemetery report strange voices and footsteps within their own walls.

On the north side of town, on the very edge of the city itself, sits Oak Hill Cemetery. Oak Hill is a beautiful, sprawling burial ground with winding paths that are perfect for a peaceful stroll. Mausoleums line the back edge, and many famous Lake Geneva legends are entombed within the cemetery itself. Oak Hill was founded in 1880, and was officially listed on the National Register of Historic Places in 2021. Construction of the cemetery was funded in part by the Sturges family, and many notable people were buried in the grounds, including the Sears family, John Moran (son of "Bugs" Moran, the notorious gangster), and 76 Civil War soldiers.

Prior to the creation of the luxurious Oak Hill grounds, Pioneer Cemetery was the site used for funerals and burials. Located just a few blocks west and north of the downtown proper, in what is now known as the Maple Park district, Pioneer opened in 1837 and was the exclusive cemetery until Oak Hill's establishment. Notable individuals buried in Pioneer include Dr. Phillip Maxwell, some twenty civil war soldiers, and many of the founding fathers of Lake Geneva, with last names familiar now as streets within the city, including LaSalle, Haskins, and Conant. Pioneer is no longer accepting burials, but is a must see slice of Lake Geneva history, tucked neatly away in a quiet neighborhood.

While there are no confirmed hauntings in either cemetery, that is not to say that strange things do not ever occur within the gates. In Oak Hill, folks who live nearby often report seeing "strange lights" that, at first, seem to be headlights of cars, but move and float in a way that makes it abundantly clear that they are not. Laughter, giggles, and strange knocking sounds have also been reported inside Oak Hill, with some locals believing that the spirits of some children buried there are willing to come and play with visitors, whether or not the visitors agree!

At Pioneer, homes that stand nearby seem to serve as a sort of "paranormal railway," with multiple former residents describing "spirits passing through." More than one person has described the phenomenon as being as though they were watching someone walking, attempting to catch a train or bus, and perhaps running late. None of the spirits seem to look the same, and none seem threatening, or like they are even aware that they are being watched. Perhaps this is related to the cemetery, or perhaps this is another "stone tape" haunting, as the old train station in Lake Geneva was just a few blocks away. Perhaps this is nothing more than a record of mundane activities, playing over and over for unsuspecting people to observe…right in their living rooms.

More sinister rumors are told about another cemetery, just on the outskirts of town. St. Kilian's Cemetery, located in Lyons Township, to the East of the city of Lake Geneva itself, has long been the source of local urban legends. Originally founded in June of 1856, the burial grounds and church were a quiet, countryside place of worship and reflection. However, in the late 1990s, the church was abandoned and fell into disrepair. It didn't take long for the locals to begin talking, and rumors of ghostly sightings, strange voices and lights, and evil misdeeds began to spread. Reports of ghostly church bells from the condemned, abandoned church were shared, as well as a strange, battery draining presence that created unease in visitors. Soon, it seemed as though everyone in the area accepted that not only was the cemetery haunted, but the church itself was being used for "satanic rituals" and other strange activities.

Of course, there's no record of any sort of devil worship happening inside the abandoned church, but the strange stories continued to spread. Local teenagers would drive their friends to the cemetery grounds to frighten each other, and strange things *were* observed by American Ghost Walks tour guide Rita Moore—who, as a teen, went to the cemetery and heard those phantom church bells, and observed dead pigeons laid on each of the windowsills of the church. Who's to say how that happened? It certainly lends to the spooky, unnerving atmosphere.

In 2002, the church itself was razed after falling into dangerous disrepair, leaving only the cemetery behind to offer strange experiences to those urban legend seekers who dare venture onto the grounds.

A MASS GRAVE OF THE FORGOTTEN

While the cemeteries inside Lake Geneva proper are full of historical wonderment and tales of legacy families, there is one site, just a few miles outside of town, that holds far more tragedy than tradition. With ties to the prolific history of healthcare in the Lake Geneva area, this site stands as a stark reminder of the conditions that the mentally ill and indigent were forced to endure because of lack of any other options.

Along County Highway NN, where today the jail, hospital, and Sheriff's Department stand, was once a large asylum known as the Walworth County Poor Farm and The Asylum for the Chronic Insane. Unlike the country club style sanitariums that stood in Lake Geneva itself, this site, tucked away into the farmlands and forest, wasn't a spot for relaxation and rejuvenation, but a work camp for those that had nowhere else to go.

First opened in 1852, the Poor Farm would become home to scores of people over the decades. If you were a poor orphan with no relatives, this is where you came. If you were a pregnant teenager abandoned by her lover and with parents who couldn't support the new addition? This is where you came. If you were too old to work and had no family to take you in, this is where you came.

Attitudes toward the impoverished were quite different in the Nineteenth Century. It was a common belief that if you were poor, it was your fault. Maybe if you worked for a while and were motivated enough, you could finally turn your life around and stop being a drain on society. Poverty was treated like a disease that you brought upon yourself and the best way to cure it was with the medicine of punishment and forced labor.

And life was even more cruel for the mentally and physically disabled. If your family couldn't take care of your needs, where else could you go? The Poor Farm was a desperate place of last resort. There was no one to provide therapy or medication. There were no accommodations for those with different bodies. We were still over a century away from the Americans with Disabilities Act.

In 1879, a wing was opened up to specifically house the insane, so they had their own space to exist with a little bit of separation from the children and the older people, and in 1917, they finally built an infirmary so that people with contagious diseases wouldn't be around healthy ones.[23] While the idea of being forced to work and do chores on a farm surrounded by people with a tenuous grip on reality and low-paid county workers with no modern medical training might seem horrific to us today, the Wisconsin State Board of Charities and Reform said in 1881 that the conditions at the Walworth County poor farm were the finest that Wisconsin had to offer.[24] And if that was the best, you can imagine the rest.

As time passed and the main buildings at the Poor Farm eventually became the Lakeland Nursing Home and the welfare state established during the Great Depression New Deal 1930s would begin helping the poor steer clear of institutions, the memory of these places begins to fade. But in 2000, a former accountant at that nursing home, Arlene Patek, and former County Surveyor Lloyd Jensen, who put up a memorial of all those lives lost to time in this place tucked away alongside a corn field.

Behind what is now Lakeland School, a plaque stands, emblazoned with hundreds of names that marks the site of a mass grave. One

---

[23] *Meandering Around Walworth County,* Ginny Hall, 1995
[24] *At The Lake,* "The Last House On The Block", Lisa Schmelz, Feb 2014

grave marker for hundreds upon hundreds of souls, all buried together, with no way of knowing whose body lies where. Best guesses estimate that bodies were dumped in the mass grave between 1879 to 1939, with only 150 of the individuals named and listed on the plaque. Of course, death struck regularly on the poor farm, particularly of the elderly where there were no families to collect the bodies, or of pregnant mothers and infants. Surviving childbirth was a tentative proposition even in wealthy families. In 1900, the infant mortality rate was 165 in 1000. That's compared to 7 out of 1000 today.[25] Babies back then were twenty-three times less likely to survive their first day than they are today and that was during some of our grandparents' lifetimes!

How many tortured souls still linger at this site, after a lifetime of misery and a death and burial that would leave any spirit with unfinished business?

And what else might linger in the sparsely inhabited woods north of Lake Geneva?

---

[25] PBS, *The First Measured Century*

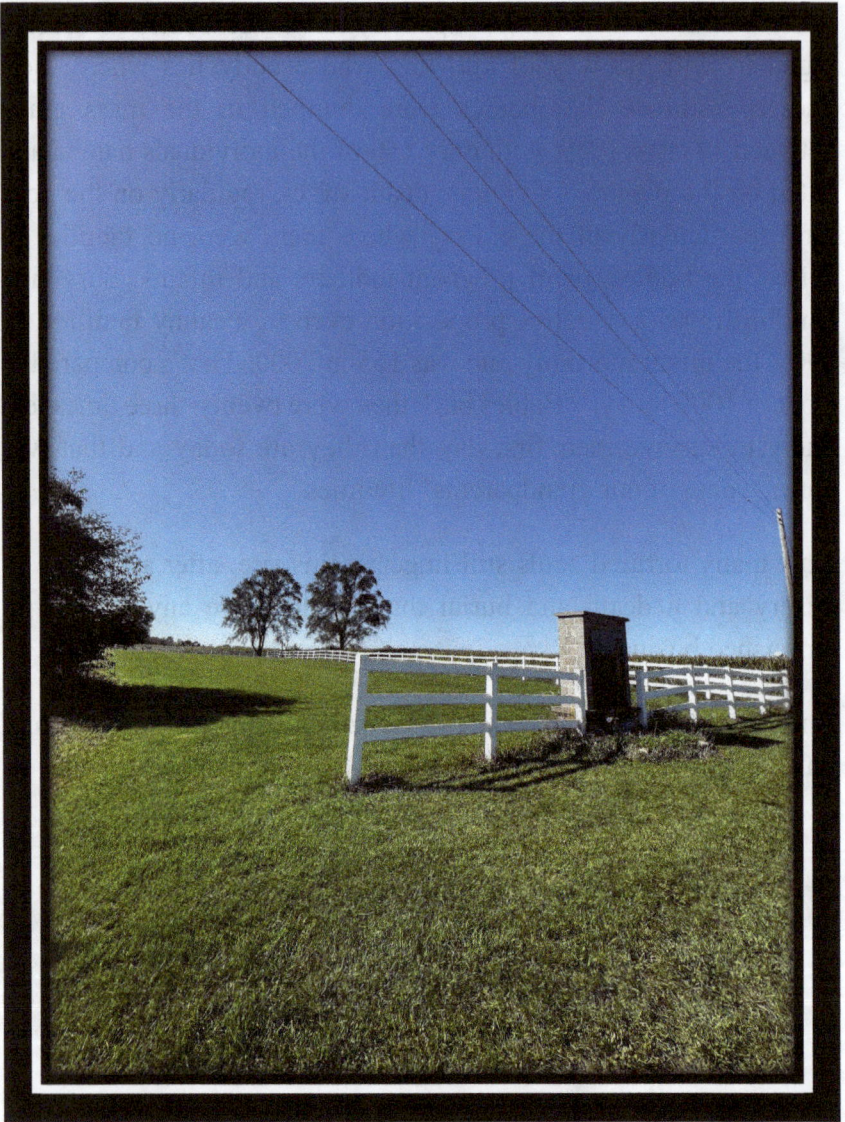

26

---

[26] Wide shot of the potter's field grave in Elkhorn, WI. Photo: Rita Mae Moore

BEAST OF BRAY ROAD

While this legend does not come from Lake Geneva itself, it's well known enough to have colored much of the Geneva Lakes area. Bray Road is a short, rural road just south of the City of Elkhorn, which is located about seven miles north of Lake Geneva itself. As it winds through farmland, seeming idyllic, the truth is that Bray Road is home to what many believe to be a terrifying beast.

The month of December is already usually a slow news season and the period between Christmas and New Year's when all the kids are out of school and on vacation is doubly so. So, when *The Week*, the local Elkhorn newspaper, ran an article about sightings of a "wolfish-looking creature that ran on two legs," it caught a lot of people's attention, so much so that it was the first edition of *The Week* to immediately sell out.

And more importantly, it launched the cryptozoology research career of Linda Godfrey. An aspiring cartoonist who got her foot in the door by offering the paper free drawings. Godfrey was added as paid staff and when one of their reporters quit, they offered her a job writing features. She had heard the rumors whispered on the school buses by the teenagers of Elkhorn of "some kind of fur-covered creature with the head of a wolf or German Shepard"[27] that walked on two legs. In the slow news time of the Holidays, Godfrey was sent on assignment to talk to the Walworth County Animal Control officer and unexpectedly, one of the most prolific and respected Twentieth Century cryptid writers emerged.

---

[27] *Monsters of Wisconsin*, Godfrey, p. 106

So, in the waning months of 1991, Linda went to talk to Jon Frederickson, that Animal Control officer and while she was there she admitted to "hemming and hawing" about asking him about the mystery creature. When she summoned the courage, Godfrey assumed he would quickly dismiss it. But Frederickson did her one better, he responded by producing a manila folder of reports labeled "Werewolf."

What Frederickson did dismiss was the idea of a dog-man running around the farm fields and backroads of Walworth County. He thought that it was just a regular wolf or coyote that had been misidentified due to the darkness and the late hour. But in his file was a list of witnesses and when Godfrey went to talk to them, they had a different story.

In her original article, Linda kept the witness Doris Gipson anonymous, using the pseudonym "Pat," a teenager who was driving on Bray Road on Halloween night of 1991 when she thought she hit a small animal about fifty yards right before the intersection of Sitler Road. As she got out of the car to investigate, she was suddenly rushed by a brown-haired beast "bigger than any animal I've ever seen around here" (but she said she didn't think it was as big as bear) and running on two legs faster than her track star uncle could possibly run (Doris had a way with creative comparisons). She got back in the car but the creature scratched her bumper with its claws and Linda even took a picture of it. Doris saw it again on the way home on the side of the road, this time with an eleven year old witness who she had been sent to pick up from trick-or-treating.

Doris' acquaintance Lori Endrizzi (anonymized as "Barbara" in the original article) had seen it two years before, holding roadkill in its arms and kneeling on the side of the road eating it. It's Lori who described things, by saying that if werewolves existed, it would have looked like what she saw. Lori's mother had also heard a howling in the night and heard from a friend of hers that he'd seen a creature like this near the creek.

The family of Karen Bowey (they didn't feel the need to be anonymous) who lived on nearby Bowers Road had also seen something. Her eleven-year old daughter Heather had seen a big dog with silver colored fur with brown in it, and it stood up on two legs and chased them towards their house before slinking back into the cornfield. Bowey thought it was just a deformed animal, but she believed her daughter.

Godfrey and her editor thought that would be it. That the article would be something for "jokes and things for a couple of weeks"[28] but that wasn't quite what happened. Soon after, people started contacting her about more sightings. Syndicated TV tabloid *Inside Edition* came to shoot a feature on the story, a British tabloid newspaper sponsored Linda to stay out all night on Bray Road with raw meat as bait. But while the national media had started to pay attention to the story, was there anything to it besides some eyewitness accounts? Could the beast be something of a paranormal nature?

One witness came forward claiming his father told him of seeing a giant dogman on a burial mound at St. Coletta's (a school and hospital about 36 miles away) in 1936 and it had said the word to him "Gadara," which was a Biblical location where Jesus cast a "legion" of demons out of a man and into a group of pigs which then jumped over a cliff and drowned. Now a talking werewolf sounds pretty supernatural.

Animal Control Officer Frederickson had already been featured in the *Milwaukee Journal* earlier in 1991 for an article about suspicious activity in an article entitled "Pets Mutilated, Cult Activity

---

[28] *See You On The Other Side* podcast, Episode 296, Dec 2021

Suspected in Linn" (a small town near Lake Geneva). The "Satanic Panic" of the 1980s hadn't quite yet subsided in southeastern Wisconsin by 1991 and it was suspected that some kind of cult had sacrificed the animals and left them for dead. But could this hungry bipedal canid (a dog that walks on two legs) have anything to do with these animal carcasses? Or if it actually was a cult, could it have anything to do with the sightings of a strange man-wolf?

To the county's credit, they quickly investigated the claims of a cult running around Southeastern Wisconsin and by the fall, the Sheriff's Department held a press conference to dismiss the rumors of Satanic activity, saying that the animal carcasses found were a "dumping ground" where people had been putting deceased animals for years and not a sacrificial site.[29]

However, most of the sightings of the Bray Road Beast that Linda investigated, stretching back to the 1960s and then throughout the 1990s and 2000s, suggest that the creature might be all too terrestrial and just a different breed of animal, perhaps a weird mutation or a family of dogs that can walk on their back legs. That would be cryptozoological, meaning a rumored physical animal whose existence is currently unproven and up until Godfrey's death in 2023, she was receiving new reports of sightings. None were as dramatic as the talking dogman of St. Coletta's, but all of them were witnessed by people convinced of the uniqueness of the creature.

Over the intervening years possible explanations have ranged from TikTokers speculating that the Beast was the Wendigo, the flesh-hungry beast that roams the Northern forests of Algonquin lore; to the more terrestrial explanation that it is a particularly large but otherwise unremarkable wolf; that it is a bear with mange; and that it is nothing more than people looking for attention. And it's

---

[29] "Reported Satanic Animal Remains Most Likely Just Dumping Ground", *Lake Geneva Regional News* June 20, 1991

certainly got attention, numerous films and books have been created, either in an attempt to explain the beast's origins like Small Town Monsters' *The Bray Road Beast*, or as more traditional horror movie fare. Famously low-budget Asylum Studios made their own creature feature inspired by the creature that roams along Bray Road in 2005. Southeastern Wisconsin's favorite cryptid has also been featured in many of the Travel Channel and Discovery Network's gallery of paranormal reality shows, such as *Lost Tapes, Expedition X,* and *In Search of Monsters.*

While tabloids across the world have loved the alliterative headline of "Wisconsin's Werewolf", some locals have embraced it as well. One home along Bray Road even erected a massive, carved wooden likeness of the beast in their front yard, complete with chains and a fence to "hold it back" (if you do drive down Bray Road to attempt your own sighting, please do not trespass on private property). An entrepreneurial high school teacher from Illinois bought a farm that buts up against Bray Road and offers hayrides where brave monster hunters can search for the Beast. Ask anyone in the Geneva Lakes area, and you will be certain to hear that if they themselves have not encountered the Beast of Bray Road…they know someone who has. Whatever it may be, it stands to reason that something strange is roaming the countryside in Walworth County, indeed.

THE END IS ONLY THE BEGINNING

So, we are left, after reading these tales, wondering about that mysterious place of "maybe." Maybe ghosts exist. Maybe Lake Geneva is teeming with supernatural activity. Or maybe it's all a trick of the mind, fed by the rich history throughout the city.

But as you walk around and experience the beauty in the area, take note. Was that simply a cool lake breeze that brushed along your neck? Or, was it something more ethereal, trying to make contact with you? How many subtle moments are we missing by not paying attention?

Next time you find yourself strolling along the Geneva lakeshore, or down a row of shops on Main Street, pause for a moment. Listen. Close your eyes and picture the centuries of history that happened all around you. Whether or not it's haunted, Lake Geneva is most assuredly full of fascination.

The spirit of the lake calls us all.

Are you listening?

SOURCES

https://atthelakemagazine.com/walk-through-pioneer-cemetery/

https://www.legendsofamerica.com/beast-of-bray-road/

https://atthelakemagazine.com/legends-snake-road/

http://www.lisaschmelz.com/yahoo_site_admin/assets/docs/Sanitar iums.167110230.pdf

https://www.lakegenevanews.net/news/geneva_lake_west/familys-tragedy-remembered-in-1895-boat-sinking/article_c44b42ab-bb5f-5321-abab-91ce0079b371.html

https://www.newspapers.com/clip/21920465/dispatch-sinking-article/

Book: Weird Wisconsin

https://www.lakegenevanews.net/opinion/columnists/chicago-fire-survivor-recounts-familys-move-to-lake-geneva/article_e7306928-6d15-5deb-9e5a-a526492331f9.html

https://jmvh.org/article/syphilis-its-early-history-and-treatment-until-penicillin-and-the-debate-on-its-origins/

https://www.socreative.club/single-post/2018/04/15/honoring-mothers-motherhood-maternal-bonds-and-the-influence-of-mothers-in-history-and-so

https://atthelakemagazine.com/last-house-on-block/ (Walworth County mass grave from asylum) https://minds.wisconsin.edu/bitstream/handle/1793/6687/Lunacy+in+the+19th+Century.pdf;jsessionid=D31DC2BAA3E6C84563015088FE3B1DCB?sequence=1 (Lunacy in the Nineteenth Century)

https://www.gygaxmemorialfund.org/lgam-35

https://en.wikipedia.org/wiki/Stone_Tape_Theory

https://lakegenevanews.net/where-troubled-folks-gathered/article_72536da2-3c07-5ece-bd34-f8fac4bcb9a5.html

https://www.psychologytoday.com/us/blog/short-history-mental-health/201311/balancing-your-humors

https://www.aamc.org/news/bloody-hands-dirty-knives-horrors-victorian-medicine

https://uploads.weconnect.com/mce/c38b4bbe8f9de63e07122b4d33d87e4ed9c9b410/St.%20Kilian%20History.pdf

https://uploads.weconnect.com/mce/c38b4bbe8f9de63e07122b4d33d87e4ed9c9b410/St.%20Kilian%20History.pdf

ACKNOWLEDGEMENTS

With Thanks—

To the many people who shared their tales with us as we researched local haunted history. To every business and home in Lake Geneva, for each individual drop in the river makes it what it is. Special thanks to the sites on the tour, for joining us in making terror and magic come alive.

To the tour guide that led the very first ghost tour that I ever went on, decades ago, lighting a fire in me that would lead me to this strange and delightful career.

To the entire American Ghost Walks family, a group of creative, motivated, charismatic individuals that are blazing trails and entertaining the heck out of people in the process.

To every person who whispered in a panicked voice, "What was that?!" and then chased after the bumps in the night.

And to every person who sets foot in Lake Geneva, because history is being written every day, and as the page turns, you are part of the story of this town, too.

ABOUT THE AUTHORS

Rita Mae Moore is a lifetime Lake Geneva area resident, with a lifetime love of history and the macabre. When she's not leading tours through historical places, she can be found dancing, writing, and spending time with her husband and three children.

Mike Huberty is the owner of tour company, American Ghost Walks, preserving and boosting haunted history across the United States. In addition, he writes songs, plays bass and sings in Weird Wisconsin rock band, Sunspot.